PRAISE FOR RICK MERCER

"Canada's most pointed political satirist for a quarter century."

—*Toronto Star*

"Mercer embodies Canada, but without the smugness."

—*The Globe and Mail*

"Week after week, Mercer continues to delight with his alternately giddy and cutting political humour."

—The Canadian Press

"The comedian of choice for viewers who read."

—*Toronto Life*

"[*A Nation Worth Ranting About*] will make you laugh out loud repeatedly."

—*The Chronicle Herald*

"Canada's leading political satirist."

—*The New York Times*

"The most fun I've had in bed for a long time."

—Shelagh Rogers, CBC, on *Rick Mercer Report: The Book*

FINAL REPORT

RICK MERCER FINAL REPORT

DOUBLEDAY CANADA

Doubleday Canada and colophon are registered trademarks of Penguin Random House Canada Limited

Library and Archives Canada Cataloguing in Publication

Mercer, Rick, 1969–, author
    Rick Mercer final report.

Issued in print and electronic formats.
ISBN 978-0-385-69247-2 (hardcover).—ISBN 978-0-385-69248-9 (EPUB)

    1. Rick Mercer report (Television program). 2. Mercer, Rick, 1969–.
3. Canada—Politics and government—2006– —Humor. 4. Canadian wit and humor (English). 5. Political satire, Canadian. I. Title. II. Title: Final report.

FC173.M465 2018   971.0702'07   C2018-902242-6
                                                 C2018-902243-4

Photo credits: page 21 (Rick with Gord Downie at the 2013 Hope Live event in Ottawa) © Jake Wright. All RMR photos © 2018 Rick Mercer.

Jacket photographs: (front) Jon Sturge; (back) © 2018 Rick Mercer
Cover and book design: Terri Nimmo

Printed and bound in the USA

Published in Canada by Doubleday Canada,
a division of Penguin Random House Canada Limited

www.penguinrandomhouse.ca

10 9 8 7 6 5 4 3 2 1

Penguin
Random House
DOUBLEDAY CANADA

To everyone who's appeared on an RMR crew list or call sheet.

Thank you.

CONTENTS

PROLOGUE:
THE END

Video Posted Online September 25, 2017

Hello everyone, Rick Mercer here. Look at me, I'm back in the alley. That can only mean one thing: We are preparing a brand-new season of the *Mercer Report*.

This alley is where I come to think. This is where I come to rant. And quite frankly, with the state of the world right now, my only concern this season is that once I start ranting, I won't be able to stop.

If you can believe it, this will be the fifteenth season of the show. And sure, it has evolved over the years, but one thing that has always remained consistent is this: I've always known that I have the best job in the country. It has been a huge privilege to be invited into your home every single week. I can't tell you how much fun it's been. So yes, this is the fifteenth season of the *Mercer Report*. It is also the final season.

What's next? I have no idea. What I do know is we have been hard at work preparing what I think will be our greatest season yet. We have just returned from an epic road trip. A lot of people say "coast to coast to coast." At the *Mercer Report*, we mean it. We've been to the Pacific. We've been to the Atlantic. We went to the Arctic Circle—I was swimming in the Arctic Ocean. I've helped paint a grain elevator on the Prairies. I've dangled off the Confederation Bridge to PEI. I have been on an intimate adventure with Jann Arden. I have been covered head to toe in peanut butter and licked clean by thirty-two golden retrievers. And why? Because when you get an invitation like that, you show up.

I love my job. I always have. I want to thank everyone who has ever watched and please, continue to do so. The *Mercer Report*, as always, CBC Television, Tuesdays at eight—eight thirty in Newfoundland and Labrador. A place where I will be spending a lot more time in the future.

INTRODUCTION:
Raise a Little Hell

"WILL RICK BE RANTING?"

This was the only question Slawko Klymkiw, the CBC's director of English-language TV programming, asked when executive producer Gerald Lunz said we were moving to Toronto with plans to launch our own show.

It was the fall of 2002, and Gerald, my partner in show business and in life, assured Slawko, "Rick will be ranting."

There were no more direct questions, which is just as well because we didn't have any answers. Details were hazy. We shook hands, and just like that, we had a TV show.

In this business, in show business, nothing happens that easily or that fast.

Rick Mercer's Monday Report launched in January of 2004, and out of the gate we had a bona fide TV hit on our hands.

Immediately, I was on the road nonstop and I loved it. The studio might have been in Toronto, but in my mind the real set for our show was the ten million square kilometres that made up the country.

We called the show *Monday Report*, a play on the title of the venerable CBC News program *Sunday Report*, a current-affairs institution. We also had an ulterior motive. From the very start, we had lobbied hard for a Monday-night time slot, the best real estate in network television. Once we'd secured that slot, we figured the best way to ensure we kept it was to put the word *Monday* in the title.

It worked like a charm. We ended our first season as the number one show on the CBC—and our champion, Slawko, promptly moved us to Tuesday. The *Monday Report* crew jackets and shirts we purchased in celebration of being renewed went to the Salvation Army and the show was rebranded simply *Rick Mercer Report*.

And I kept ranting.

But from the moment we were renewed, I had one nagging fear: Would I have enough to rant about? We had a hit on our hands, and that was exciting, but in TV a hit can run for five to seven years. How would I find something to rant about every week?

Eventually, I learned not to underestimate the absurdity of life in this confederation we call Canada.

My cameraman, Don Spence, who was there for every rant and every adventure for fifteen years, has done the math. Together we walked forty-two kilometres in Graffiti Alley— me marching forward with a chip on my shoulder, Don marching backward, a forty-five-pound camera on his.

I never did run out of subjects to rant about. And while the rants didn't really change in style, they did change in tone.

When I started, my motto was "Anger is my cardio." It still stands as my single-line bio on my Twitter feed. It is a tad disingenuous. I don't consider myself an angry person. That's Gerald's job.

Sure, some of the rants came from an angry place—there is a lot to be angry about. If you watched Question Period every day, like I used to, being anything but angry would probably be a sign of dissociative mental disorder. But I am not for the most part an angry person. I do, however, believe there is nothing to be gained by keeping quiet or pretending that everything is fine when it is clearly not.

We all know those people. The curtains in the living room are on fire and their response is "Well, there are *some* flames, and yes, there is smoke, and it seems to be moving up the wall, but if we just take our drinks and move to the kitchen, I think everything will be fine."

Where there is smoke, the couch is on fire; where there is an absurdity in life, or an injustice, or a point of view that needs exploring, there should be a rant. And when government decides it can get away with treating the electorate like idiots and fools, there should be a lot of rants from a lot of people.

I love a funny rant. I love it when I can sense the audience at home saying *"Exactly!"* all at the same time. I loved it when I had the opportunity to rant about an issue of national importance, like when it became evident to me that a huge chunk of the Canadian population didn't know the correct way to use an escalator. They seemed to be under the impression it was a ride at Canada's Wonderland, not a way to move everyone forward. For God's sake, people—stand on the right, walk up the left. Rules of the road.

Over time, I came to realize that a rant did not have to be funny or ironic or angry. Sometimes, something just needs to be said. When it is your job to talk about what is on your mind, the country's mind, and Gord Downie passes away, you talk about Gord Downie.

Ranting has been a passion of mine for as long as I can remember. I come from an island of ranters. I love the process of taking a subject that is large and complex and distilling it into a single, coherent, ninety-second rant.

Every Thursday night in my office for fifteen seasons, I would write. I would free-associate on my subject until I had everything I wanted to say down on paper. The initial draft would inevitably be ten to 12 pages long. I would then review the stack of pages and think the same thing: "How the hell am I going to get this one down to ninety seconds?" Then I would start the process: cut the fat, put it on simmer, and repeat.

If I were being romantic, I would say that the process of crafting a rant is not much different from taking an entire cow and reducing it to a single cup of gravy—which, as any Newfoundlander will tell you, is a beverage that's good for the soul.

Looking back now, the show that we produced every week for fifteen years looked very much like the one we proposed to Slawko a decade and a half earlier. The rants were there—250 of them over 250 shows. And certainly the travel was there—no nook or cranny went unexplored, from sea to sea to sea and back again five hundred times.

Originally, when we were mulling over a theme song for the first episode, I suggested "Raise a Little Hell" by Trooper. For me it's the ultimate Canadian rock and roll song, guaranteed to get you a speeding ticket. The Canadian Rant set to music.

But we wanted the show to emulate a current-affairs program, not the soundtrack to my basement in grade eight. So we went to the brilliant composer Ed Eagan. Gerald had one note for Ed: "This has to feel like a current-affairs show, so the theme music has to create a false sense of urgency."

Ed delivered, and we never looked back. The theme never changed.

That said, on April 10, 2018, when I signed off the air and said goodnight for the last time, under the credits, "Raise a Little Hell" played. And boy, was I proud.

If you don't like what you see, why don't you fight it?
If you know there's something wrong, why don't you right it?
Raise a little hell . . .

That's what we did.

Shooting with Justin Trudeau in Quebec City. A great day—until this big guy attacked us and choked us out. We both went three minutes without oxygen. Explains a lot.

If it's Tuesday that means I am shooting with the navy off the coast of British Columbia.

Black tie and tails at the Calgary Zoo.

NET GAIN

April 3, 2018

Visiting the schools in the Spread the Net Student Challenge is always the highlight of my year. Trust me, if you are remotely pessimistic about anything at all, that is the cure. Just try to remain a glass-half-empty guy when you roll into a town like Peterborough, Ontario, and you meet a young woman in grade eleven who donated her entire pay-cheque from Red Lobster to Spread the Net.

Or if you want to feel good about the future or the next generation, consider this: Last year, the school that raised more money than any other school in Canada was in Fort McMurray, Alberta. You could still smell the smoke from the wildfires in the air. Less than one year after every kid in that school was evacuated from their town, their homes and their beds—they were back, and they were raising money so that kids on the other side of the planet could sleep safely at night.

I look forward to these back-to-school visits the same way some people look forward to a vacation down south. A great place to visit, but I wouldn't want to live there. Because let's face it: School is hard. I don't mean math-class hard. I mean figuring-out-the-world hard. And students today have got to deal with stuff we didn't even imagine possible. And yet they not only survive, but they thrive. And they do it with compassion and they do it with tolerance.

I can only speak about my generation, but this crowd, compared to us, are not only smarter than we were, they're nicer too. The media will always tell us that kids today are entitled. On that point, I will agree. They are entitled to a better country and a better world. And from what I've seen, this generation is going to make that happen.

.

SINISTER MEDIA
March 27, 2018

Recently I decided I wanted to buy a curling rock. I'm not a curler—it was a passing fancy. So I went on Kijiji and checked. There were no used curling rocks in my area. So I did a Google search for curling rocks for sale in Canada. And sure enough, there they were. But they cost between seven hundred and eight hundred bucks. I had no idea they were so expensive. I remember thinking, "Well, why's that?" Then I closed that window and forgot all about it.

The very next day on my Facebook feed, a friend—who turned out to be fake—posted an article entitled WHY ARE CURLING ROCKS SO EXPENSIVE? I'd never even said those words out loud—I'd just thought them in my head. And then Instagram started telling me to follow all of these curlers. Then I was in Gmail and I got a pop-up ad saying I should go join a gay curling league.

The truth is, I have no real interest in curling. I was going to use the rock as a doorstop on my balcony. 'Cause, you know, it's got a handle.

Why is it that we're surprised that the forces of evil will

use Facebook and social media to manipulate elections when a simple Google search will do everything but show up at your house and personally drag you off to the gay curling league? All the big internet players—Facebook, Amazon, Google, Satan—say the same thing: they will self-police; they will protect our privacy; they will try not to disrupt democracy. Not gonna happen. Unless they are regulated, they will run rampant. And when that happens, all we can do is unplug everything.

Sadly, these companies know that for most of us, no matter what the stakes, unplugging is far too high a price to pay.

Now, if you will excuse me, I have to go talk to a man named Brad about what to wear to the bonspiel.

THE OFFICIAL MONEY PIT

March 20, 2018

Twenty-four Sussex Drive is the official residence of Canada's prime minister. It is also a rundown, drafty barn. Eleven prime ministers refused to maintain the place. It is a barely standing testament to the fact that prime ministers will allow something we own to crumble and fall apart around them in order to make themselves look good.

It took Justin Trudeau to come along and say, "Okay, the place is filled with mould and lead—I'm not raising my children there." Typical Liberal. When Stephen Harper lived there he claimed his daily mould and lead intake made him stronger.

Now we find out there's more asbestos in that pile than anticipated. Way more. It was supposed to cost ten million to renovate. Now it might cost thirty million. Then there are the problems no amount of money could possibly fix. From a security point of view, the place is a disaster. The front door of the residence is literally a stone's throw away from a public street. A drunk on the sidewalk could hit a visiting dignitary in the head with a can of soup. That's no good.

When the decision was made to make it the official residence, it was a friendlier, nicer time. Back then the biggest nightmare the RCMP had was that someone would put a flaming bag of poo on the front step, ring the doorbell and run away. A prank that both John Diefenbaker and Lester B. Pearson fell for many times. My, how the children laughed.

Times have changed, and so must we. It's time to tear the place down, build a brand-new, secure structure. The coolest, greenest, funkiest residence we can. It's our house. We're a grown-up country. We can have nice things.

SHUT DOWN THE SUPERSHARKS

March 13, 2018

Yﾻou've got to hand it to them: They certainly seem like nice people. The payday loan people. They advertise nonstop. Their commercials are constantly on the radio and the television. They've got those catchy jingles that were written by Satan himself so they enter your head and just stay there forever. You need cash? You need money? They've got cash *and* money. The business model is very simple: If you show up and you're upright and you've got air in one lung, they'll give you money.

The terms are incredibly generous—or at least they seem that way. Say you're in Ontario, say you want a thousand bucks. They'll give you a thousand bucks. But they'll charge you fifteen bucks for every hundred bucks. Now, math is not my high suit, but even *I* can figure this out. Fifteen bucks on a hundred bucks, that's 15 percent. That sounds pretty good. Except it's not. Because it's 15 percent *every two weeks*. Thanks to the miracle of compound interest, that's an annual interest rate of 390 percent.

They are giving cash advances to the poorest, most vulnerable people in society and charging an annual interest rate of 390 percent. Loansharking is 60 percent. I would call them weasels, except weasels have a moral compass. Every province has tried to regulate this industry, and still they manage to find ways to operate. Kind of the way that poison gas will fit under the crack of any door. It's time for the federal government to get serious here. Forget the regulations, seal their doors, shut them down.

GO, CANADA!

March 6, 2018

Okay, sports fans, we are just two days away from the opening of the Paralympics in Pyeongchang.

I have been very lucky in my job. I've probably met and played with close to a hundred Paralympians. I have been beaten by, humiliated by and inspired by Canadian athletes missing every combination of limb you could possibly imagine. If you are an able-bodied person and you have never really tucked in and watched the Paralympics, you've got to do this. There's stuff going on there you didn't even know was possible. Guys like John Leslie, Canadian champion snowboarder. Dude had his foot and ankle amputated. They took that, they laid that over there for later, and then they took off his remaining leg above the knee. Then they reattached the foot and ankle where the knee used to be, except backwards! His foot and ankle now function as a knee. Which he snowboards on— very fast—for Canada.

Then there's the sledge hockey guys. Those guys are only happy when they're slamming into one another. You get Canada versus USA in sledge hockey, it is fast, it is furious. To the uninitiated, it looks like a group of paraplegics doing everything in their power to become quadriplegics. We are two days out from an amazing Games. Canada's Paralympic team—there's no tougher and no finer. And like all great Olympians, they make for great TV.

DEEP END OF THE GANGES

February 27, 2018

J ustin Trudeau and his family have returned from a whirlwind eight-day visit to India. Despite some adorable family pictures on Instagram, I think it's safe to say things got a little weird over there.

When the Beatles went to India and hung out with the Maharishi Yogi, things got freaky too, but they had an excuse: They were swallowing tabs of LSD like they were Glosettes.

It is one thing to dip your toe in the culture that you are visiting, but the Trudeaus dove into the deep end of the Ganges. They did not come up for air. They had a traditional Indian outfit picked out for every single day of the week. At one point Justin showed up in public wearing the outfit of a traditional Indian groom. And Sophie was his traditional Indian bride. Who does that? I'll tell you who does it: Indian people. On their wedding day. Not two visitors from Montreal. When the prime minister of Japan shows up in Canada, he does not get off the plane wearing his Anne of Green Gables wig and his peasant dress. No, that's for private time.

Of course, it wasn't all dress-up in India; there was also, unfortunately, official business. Marred by the fact that the Prime Minister's Office accidentally invited a convicted attempted murderer to a dinner and a reception. Now, this guy is Canadian, he shot an Indian cabinet minister, and our government invited him to a reception in India. How does that happen?

Governing is supposed to be serious business. And yet despite all this, some people are calling the trip a success. Yes, I guess if you judge success by the number of likes you get on Instagram. My fear is that for this government, those likes are good enough.

FOCUS ON THE OLYMPICS

February 6, 2018

I have on many occasions put on gear and hung out with and even trained with Olympians and Paralympians. For a guy who consistently failed to medal in the Canada Fitness Award Program in school, it has been an unexpected honour. But after meeting so many of these elite athletes up close, I have to tell you: It may look like a glamorous life, but it is not.

I have never met a group of people who so routinely make so many personal sacrifices for their job. And they start so young. At a time when most people are navigating grade eight, they basically put any semblance of a normal life on hold so they can devote all their time and energy to one thing. Then they spend the rest of their formative years doing that one thing over and over again with one goal in mind: representing us—representing Canada—at the Olympics. The only break they ever have in their schedule is occasionally they'll be asked to pee in a cup by a total stranger. They redefine commitment.

Look at snowboarder Mark McMorris. How good is this guy? He is the first snowboarder in the world to land a backside triple cork 1440. I don't even know what that is, but I am in awe of this guy. Less than a year ago, he hit a tree and broke his arm, his ribs, his pelvis and his jaw. I think it's safe to say that if that happened to any of us, we might take a break from downhill sports. Not Mark McMorris. He is in Pyeongchang, Korea, right now with one goal in mind: making us proud.

When it comes to the Winter Olympics and Team Canada, the division of labour is crystal clear: They do all the work, we do the cheering. Now let's do our job so they can do theirs.

TIME TO REBOOT
January 30, 2018

I can't tell you how many times in my life I have been in awe of modern technology. High-speed internet, smart phones . . . we live in amazing times. The advancements have been incredible to watch. But you know what? I think we should stop now. I think we were heading in the right direction, but somewhere we got lost. It used to be that you'd turn on your computer, you'd use your computer, it was great, and that was that. Now I turn on my computer, the first thing it does is tell me it's going to turn itself off, reboot and then download a system upgrade that will take twenty minutes to an hour, depending on its mood.

Phones are worse. If you have an iPhone it needs to be updated more often than a baby needs to be changed. My phone threatens me like a mob boss. It tells me if I don't accept the upgrade, bad things will happen. So you accept the upgrade—next thing you know, your battery doesn't last as long and you're getting traffic updates you never wanted.

Everything about technology that was supposed to help us is now starting to torture us. Remember when Siri first came along? She was helpful and interesting. She liked my questions. Now she's like a drunk who makes no sense. She gets angry and defensive if you ask her what the date is.

Yes, technology is more efficient now than it ever was, but instead of giving us more free time (its original purpose), it's more demanding on our time. It's enslaving us. And really, I don't know what we're going to do about it because, honestly, I can't imagine living any other way.

JUSTIN, ANDREW AND JAGMEET

January 23, 2018

Justin Trudeau is a very lucky politician. Nothing sticks to this guy. He goes out there on the road, doing all these town halls all over Canada. He gets up there in front of big crowds. He totally goes off script and starts freewheeling it. And yes, sometimes it works. But man, when he's in improv mode, some of the stuff that comes out of his mouth is baffling. At this point, I wouldn't be surprised if his lips parted and a Tide detergent pod popped out.

Now, you would think the opposition would be all over this, but let's face it: Nobody can pick those guys out of a lineup. Andrew Scheer, the new Conservative leader . . . well, he's a really nice guy. I know this because the party keeps releasing videos telling us that he's a really nice guy. The last video had Andrew telling us that when he was growing up, Dad didn't have a car, so he had to take the bus to school. I have not been so inspired by a tale of a young man overcoming personal adversity since Rick Hansen got in the wheelchair and went all the way around the globe. Andrew, here's an idea: Next time you release a video, put some policy in it. You may be afraid of policies, but Canadians are not.

Then we have the NDP. You might have missed this, but they, too, have a brand new leader: Jagmeet Singh. He held a big event last week, invited the media, and they all showed up because they thought he might be announcing policy. Nope! He wanted the media there so they could watch while he asked his girlfriend to marry him. Yeah. That happened. Jagmeet, I know some people propose marriage in public. Sometimes they do it in front of strangers. Some people do it on the Jumbotron at a hockey game and yes, Canadians clap for them, but trust me, Jagmeet: We don't vote for those people.

Justin Trudeau is a very lucky man, but luck can't last forever in politics. Although with opposition like this, it just might.

DOUBLE TROUBLE

January 16, 2018

Six months ago, if you asked random Canadians on the street what they thought about Tim Hortons, the vast majority of them would probably have said positive things. In this country we've always had time for Tim Hortons. So it is inconceivable that Tim Hortons is suddenly front and centre in the debate on how companies treat minimum-wage employees. I would say that the guy who built Tim Hortons is spinning in his grave, except he's still very much alive. That would be Ron Joyce Sr., the genius who built the Tim Hortons empire—an iconic brand that most Canadians felt reflected Canadian values. That's Ron *Senior*. Do not confuse him with Ron Jr.

Ron Jr. is the son. Kind of like Fredo in *The Godfather*. Ron Jr. is also in the Tim Hortons business. He owns two stores up in Cobourg, Ontario. In his spare time he sits around in Florida and comes up with cost-saving measures designed to improve the Tim Hortons experience—not for the customers or the employees, but, you know, for the owners. People like him.

For example, this past Christmas Ron Jr. came up with the idea that from now on his employees at Tim Hortons who make minimum wage—when they work a nine-hour shift, he will only pay them for eight hours and twenty minutes. You see, he's upset about this increase in the minimum wage, so he thought he would make a point on the backs of his employees. You've got to hand it to Junior: He is very committed to his work. It is not easy to destroy the Tim Hortons brand. It's exhausting. Especially in the Florida heat.

If you ever wondered why we need minimum labour standards in this country, look no further. Leave it up to some of these owners, and every Hortons in the country would be staffed by grandmothers doing twelve-hour shifts for payment in tea bags. It's time that Tim Hortons realized people are now watching. And if Tim's doesn't do a U-turn fast, customers in their drive-through just might.

A RINK TO RILE THEM ALL

December 5, 2017

It's pretty much unanimous among the media, the pundits, the opposition: Everyone is upset about this hockey rink that's opening on Parliament Hill. If you look at the coverage, you'd swear it's not a hockey rink at all, but a crime against humanity.

If you're not familiar with the story, log on and look at the Parliament Hill webcam—it's practically my home page. It's an amazing image. The government of Canada has gone out and built a temporary outdoor hockey rink, complete with bleachers and boards. It's just sitting there on the lawn of the Parliament Buildings.

Now, of course, people are upset that, because it's the government, it cost a whack of cash. Also, because it's the government, there are all these government kind of rules: you can't text and skate at the same time; you can't slam pucks off the boards during family skating. People are also upset because the government's going to spend about a million bucks bringing in peewee hockey teams from all over Canada for a tournament.

Look, I don't live in Ottawa. Like the vast majority of Canadians, I am never going to see this thing in person. And you know what? I still love it. I can't help myself. I think it looks cool.

And the image of ten-year-olds playing hockey on the Hill, that's going to be seen all over the world. A world in which, sadly, far too many houses of government are wrapped in barbed wire and machine guns. And in this joyous holiday season, if Canada is seen as a place where ten-year-olds can skate in the shadow of the Peace Tower, what's not to love?

CENSOR CENSURE

November 28, 2017

Wilfrid Laurier University was in the news last week, and sadly not because the Laurier Golden Hawks have won three provincial curling championships in a row. Nope. They dragged a teaching assistant over the coals for the egregious crime of showing an interview in her classroom that had originally aired on public television. The idea being, the students would watch the interview and then discuss the content. It's a slippery slope. You allow that kind of thing to go on at a university, the next thing you know, they will be drowning kittens.

The amazing thing about this story is not that it's so absurd; it's that it's happening so often. Every time we turn around we hear about discussion and debate being disallowed in a university because someone is offended. Speaking of which, the offending video in the Laurier story is an interview with a guy who, in my opinion, is an irritating dinosaur on some silly crusade against gender-neutral pronouns. How do I have this opinion? I watched the video. I don't agree with the guy in the video, but I'm glad I watched it.

But more important, I'm very glad that a so-called institute of higher learning is not in charge of what I can and cannot watch. If that were the case, I wouldn't have an opinion; I'd be ignorant. Which I guess would make me the ideal student of the future. All universities should be paying very close attention to this. Because the idea that young adults cannot be exposed to unpopular opinion in the classroom—that's an idea that's about as dangerous as an idea can get.

MINIMUM IS NOT ENOUGH

November 21, 2017

In about half of the provinces of this country, there is a scenario unfolding. Some would call it a nefarious plot that could lead to economic devastation and a complete breakdown in social order. I'm talking about an increase in the minimum wage.

To hear the experts talk about it, you'd swear it was going to lead to the end of civilization as we know it. The Ontario Chamber of Commerce are so flipped out about this, they have been on a tour of the province for about a year. They roll into a town and invite local business leaders down to the ballroom of a hotel—it's always during the workday. They charge between sixty and 130 bucks a seat. And they all sit around and talk about what a bad idea it would be if the waiter—that guy over there holding thirty-five pounds of seared chicken and butternut squash on a tray—gets a tiny raise. It's an irony-free zone.

In my family there's a young man who works stocking shelves in a supermarket. He works nights. He only works nights because he gets an extra buck twenty an hour to do so. One dollar and twenty cents an hour above minimum wage. He gives up access to daylight and members of the opposite sex for a buck twenty. Why? Because he's poor. He's the working poor. He is doing everything he can to get ahead. But he's not. If it weren't for family, he would be sunk.

Small and medium-sized businesses are the economic engine of this country. But to run an engine you need gas in the tank. And you need a workforce that at least has a chance of surviving in this world. Right now, minimum-wage earners—they're not coming close.

JUST DON'T, JASON

November 14, 2017

When I was a teenager I didn't know a single gay person. As far as I was concerned, I was the only gay dude within a hundred miles in every direction.

For a young person, that's a very difficult situation in which to find yourself. When I was in high school there was certainly no such thing as a gay-straight alliance. Thank God we had the drama club, which basically turned out to be the same thing.

Now there are gay-straight alliances (GSAs) all over Canada. And in Alberta there's Bill 24. This is legislation that tells schools they are not to pick up the phone and call parents and inform them if a student is seen attending a GSA meeting. Now, you may ask why anyone would need legislation like that. I'll tell you why. You remember Jason Kenney? He was banging around Ottawa for decades. Well, now he's back.

Jason made a name for himself nationally as a loud, proud activist against same-sex marriage. Although you can't really blame the guy for that. We're talking about the olden days, way back in 2005. And for a fella like Jason, the epitome of old-school masculinity, the notion of two fellas getting married was enough to give him the vapours. And lesbians? That's the stuff of Jason's nightmares.

Now, imagine Jason's shock when, after twenty years in Ontario, he returns to run Alberta for them and finds out they've had GSAs there for years now. So it was Jason who said the schools should tell the parents if a kid attends a GSA meeting. In much the same way that parents are contacted immediately if a student shows any interest in joining the school's newspaper or, God forbid, the improv club—both activities that will lead to a lifetime of confusion.

This is all about outing young people, and it is serious because there is a very good chance that Jason Kenney will be the next premier of Alberta. Jason: Stop it. Stick to playground rules. Pick on someone your own size.

CHEQUES AND BALANCES

November 7, 2017

This past October 31 marked not just Halloween but exactly one year to the day since the Liberals promised to finally fix the Phoenix payroll system. For those of you not up to speed, Phoenix is a payroll system designed to pay every single Canadian civil servant. The Conservatives spent $307 million inventing this thing. Unfortunately, it didn't work—it was total junk. So the Liberals came along, and they spent $400 million fixing it. Right now—and this is a technical evaluation—as far as payroll systems go, it's about as effective as a grade ten dropout with nine fingers and a serious buzz on.

There are people who work for you and me—say, for the Coast Guard or the Department of National Defence—who have not been paid for months and months. There are people being underpaid, people being overpaid, people being told that they are deceased. And the amazing thing is that, apparently, there's nothing that can be done about it. What has happened to us? We're not talking about colonizing Mars here. This is a payroll system. These things have been around forever.

During World War I, half a million Canadian men walked through storefronts, turned their heads, coughed and just like that they were in the army. Then they put their name on a piece of paper and they could check a box if they wanted to send a portion of their wages home to mom, a sweetheart or that waitress in Halifax. And then they went off to war, and guess what happened? They got paid, every single month, by the Canadian government. Did I mention there was a war on?

One hundred years later, every single possible mistake that can happen to a paycheque is happening, but in record speed with maximum efficiency. If this is what passes for progress in government, we need a lot less artificial intelligence and a few more real brains.

THE ART OF DEALING WITH TRUMP

October 17, 2017

Prime minister of Canada is a great gig. If you're going to be the leader of a country, it doesn't get much better than Canada. We have so much going for us. One of our greatest assets actually has nothing to do with us at all, but rather the stellar quality of our neighbours. And every prime minister since Mackenzie King could count on that.

But that's the thing about great neighbours, isn't it? You think they're gonna be there forever, and then one day there's a "sold" sign out front and you're living next door to an angry accordion player who gets drunk and wanders out into the backyard naked and argues with squirrels. That actually happened to a friend of mine.

When I watch Justin Trudeau on the world stage with Donald Trump discussing bilateral trade, I think of my friend. Because when you look in Justin's eyes when he's standing there next to Donald and Melania, he's smiling, but you can tell he's totally waiting for the President to drop his pants and whip out an accordion. As he said, Canada must be prepared for anything.

I admire the Prime Minister's approach. He's a better man than me. When my friend got the nutty neighbour, my advice was to turn the hose on him. But my friend said no. And he took a diplomatic approach. And no matter what happened next door, he refused to engage. And this went on for years. But this past winter: breakthrough! They went halves on a snow blower. Because it made sense to both parties.

So good luck, Prime Minister. Fingers crossed, Canada. Steady as she goes.

GORD

October 10, 2017

It's been a week now since Gord Downie, lead singer of the Tragically Hip, passed away. The outpouring of emotion from all across Canada is like nothing I've ever seen before in my life. In fact, it was so big, it was so grand, that three days in, I half expected Gord to show up on *The National* and announce another tour.

Seventeen years ago I got a call from Gord Downie. Still one of the greatest phone calls I've ever gotten in my life. It was a very short call. He was recording a song and he wanted to know if he was saying the name of a town in Newfoundland, which he had put in a lyric, the way a Newfoundlander would say it: Isle aux Morts. I said, "Yes, that sounds right to me. But if you want a second opinion, you can always call my dad." And I gave him the number. Then I forgot all about it.

A week later Dad says, "Your friend Gord called. He

wanted to know all about the time I took you and your brother camping near Isle aux Morts and we went fishing there. And he wanted to know all about the time I worked with the Department of Fisheries on the salmon rivers in central Newfoundland. And he wanted to know all about growing up in Bay Roberts. Seems like a great guy. We talked for about an hour." I said, "Dad, do you have any idea who that was? That's Gord Downie. He's the lead singer of Canada's greatest rock and roll band. He's one of our greatest songwriters." And Dad said, "Really? He never mentioned he was in a band. He just said it was Gord from Kingston."

Six months later, I walk into my parents' place and on the coffee table, there's this beautiful print of a bird next to a lake. I'm like, "Dad, this is the artwork from the new Tragically Hip album." He said, "Really? I didn't know that. Your friend Gord sent it to me." It was an original silkscreened print.

I didn't know Gord Downie that well, but I'm gonna miss him like I knew him very well. We all will. Because as an artist, he spoke to each one of us directly. And he could do that because he listened to people like my dad.

NETFLIX IS EXCEPTIONAL

October 10, 2017

So much fanfare, hoopla and dare I say flimflammery this past month with the Liberal announcement that Netflix, instead of paying taxes in Canada, will spend five hundred million dollars, over five years, making TV shows and films here. Okay, let's just back that up. Instead of paying taxes?

Netflix's opening position is: We do not have a physical presence in Canada; therefore we will not pay taxes in Canada. Wow! That's a clever trick. If you or I want to sell widgets in Canada, we have to pay taxes. Even if they are virtual widgets. If anyone wants to do business in Canada, they have to pay taxes—that's how we pay for hospitals and roads and the wonderful work of the Winnipeg Ballet.

I believe it was Benjamin Franklin about two hundred years ago who said, and I'm paraphrasing, the only two things in this world you cannot avoid are death and taxes. He did not add, "unless you're streaming old episodes of *Law and Order.*"

And as far as the five hundred million dollars they say they're going to spend here—they do that anyway. Television and film companies from all over the world shoot in Canada because we have good crews, a low dollar, and BC looks like twelve different planets.

I love Netflix and I've had it since day one. But they're not a religion, they're not a not-for-profit. When the $10.99 comes off my Visa, I am well aware that I am purchasing a service and not making a donation to World Vision. Okay, so they make a lot of money. I'm happy for them. Profit is good. But Netflix, if you want to operate in Canada, contribute to Canada just like everybody else.

GRID BLOCK

October 3, 2017

I have a picture in my telephone of a Ford F-150 pickup truck blocking an entire intersection. I watched as he slowly entered a crowded intersection, on a yellow light, knowing full well he was not going to make it all the way through. His light turned red—*boom*, he was stuck. My light turned green, but could I move forward? No, of course not, because thanks to him, *I* was stuck. Everyone behind me, they were stuck too. Total gridlock in all four directions.

People were getting frustrated; people were late for dinner; carbon flowed into the atmosphere; kidneys were not getting to the OR on time—all because of that guy. And the guy just sat there with that look on his face that was like, "Yup, here I am blocking an intersection, ruining everyone's day, and I don't care."

Look, traffic is a real problem in this country. We've all spent too much time stuck in it. Yes, experts have all sorts of theories on how to improve it, but if you want a solution, one that's not going to cost money, one that's going to *make* money, this is it: Make the people who block the intersection pay. Make them pay a lot. All of them. And there are a ton of them. This is a gold mine in narcissism.

Hire someone to stand on the corner during rush hour, and if someone puts their big, stupid minivan in the middle of an intersection and blocks traffic, issue them a large, prohibitive fine. Except we do not call it a fine, we can call it what it is: a "Yes, everyone hates you" tax. If you want to act like you're the only person on the planet, pay for the privilege.

BLAME THE BOGEYMAN

September 26, 2017

I t is a political truth in this country that we do not elect governments; we like to throw governments out. It's been about two years now since we took a look at Stephen Harper and his blue meanies and threw them out the door. It is another political truth in this country that new governments, around the two-year mark, tend to lose perspective on how and why they got elected in the first place.

Which is why the Liberals are suddenly under the misguided assumption that they're in power not because we threw the blue meanies out, but because everyone fell in love with Liberals and everything they stand for. They think they're in power solely because they are the smartest, most competent, most beautiful people in all the land. No, Justin. No. You're what's called the booby prize. Canadians looked at you during the last election and said, "Hey, look at him! He can walk and talk at the same time. He will do." Then we biffed the old guy out. "Sunny ways," you said. "Bring it on," we said.

Which leads us to our current situation regarding the Liberals' decision to make small business the new Canadian bogeyman. Why? I'll tell you why. Because small business is up to no good. Small-business owners are getting away with stuff. The details are shady, but this government, this cabinet, is committed to putting an end to it.

Remember the good old days when the Tories would just blame everything on the elites? They couldn't even say who the elites were, but it was all their fault. The Liberals are doing the exact same thing. They're just swapping one bogeyman—the elites—for a new one: small business. Let's not forget their latest bogeyman: farmers. Really, Justin? Farmers?

You want proof that a government is starting to lose its ways, see if they'll pick a fight with farmers. Why would they do such a thing? I have no idea. Maybe Liberals are against vegetables. In the ground, I mean. Not in cabinet.

DISTRACTOR-IN-CHIEF

March 21, 2017

Politicians love to change the channel when things aren't going their way. That said, it's easier said than done. You can't just snap your fingers and convince the entire world to stop talking about one thing and then start talking about something else. Or at least that used to be the case before Donald Trump.

I hate to say this, but nobody changes the channel quite like Trump. It's like he's got the magic remote control. You will not find that guy sitting around praying for a natural disaster to save him. Because when he tweets, people go berserk. They read the tweet, go into a full-body spasm and their eyes start rolling in the backs of their heads. They do everything but wet themselves. Every one of his tweets is talked about, analyzed, mocked and ridiculed.

But do you know what people *aren't* talking about? What he's doing for the other twenty-three hours a day when he's not playing with his phone. They announced drilling in national parks. Did anyone notice? Hard to tell because that's also when he tweeted that Meryl Streep was overrated as an actress. Please, Mr. President, have you seen *Sophie's Choice*?

He's stopped funding the removal of toxic waste from the Great Lakes. Was the left outraged? Hard to tell; mostly they were appalled because he tweeted about Snoop Dogg. He's cut off all money allocated to fight the Asian carp. Google "Asian carp," people—it's like every single alien-invasion movie ever made. But is anyone talking about the carp? No sir, because OMG, he tweeted about Schwarzenegger again.

Every time you hear someone say, "Did you see what Trump tweeted?" it's all going according to his plan. It has often been said that politicians will sell their souls if they could just get away with murder. Turns out no sale required; all you need is a Twitter account.

JUDGING CONSENT

March 14, 2017

Not that long ago a judge in Alberta asked a nineteen-year-old woman, in the middle of an assault trial, why she just didn't keep her knees together. Now, I say "not that long ago" because it's important to point out that this happened in 2014 and not 1957. And I admit, when it did happen, when it was in the newspapers, I thought, "This is a proverbial case of one bad apple; we're dealing with one out-of-touch judge." I may have been suffering under the delusion of white male privilege.

Conservative leader Rona Ambrose felt differently. She introduced a bill, demanding that before anyone else becomes a judge, they have to take a class explaining to them what sexual assault is. Well, legal experts were deeply insulted. After all, *they're* the experts—not the politicians. Telling them they need a refresher course on the law is like telling an astronaut they need to go to Young Drivers before they go off into space.

As it turns out, all those experts were wrong. Rona was right. And judges in this country seem to be going out of their way to prove it over and over again. In Newfoundland we have a court that seems completely confused as to what consent actually means. In Nova Scotia there's a judge who seems to be saying, "Maybe no means no, but blacked out and blind drunk? Well, that's a definite yes."

Rona is right. But she's half-right. Because it's not the future judges I'm wondering about; it's the ones we have now that seem to be causing all the trouble. Every single one of them should pop by Shoppers Drug Mart and pick up some pencils and do what Rona says: go back to school.

QUITTIN' TIME
March 7, 2017

As you may or may not know, fourteen people are running for the leadership of the Conservative Party of Canada. Who am I kidding? The chances of anyone actually knowing anything about this race are very slim. It hasn't really captured the imagination of the public. I had just one wish for the Conservative Party—and no, it's not what you were thinking. I was hoping that, for the sake of this once-great political machine, whoever was running for the leadership would be able to string a sentence together or articulate a vision for the future.

No such luck.

I have watched all of the debates. If you haven't, that's fine. Why would you? Or better yet, *how* could you? The Ottawa debate was held at three o'clock on a Friday afternoon. Who has time to watch a debate at three o'clock on a Friday afternoon? The only people who watched were myself, Rosie Barton and a handful of Northern shut-ins.

It is clear that half the candidates are not in it for Canada; they're in it for themselves. They just want to hear their own voices and see their own names in the newspaper. Which is fine, but that's what community theatre is for.

If this party wants to create any excitement, if it wants to start having real debates, it needs to streamline. May I suggest that each of the candidates look at themselves in the mirror and ask three deeply personal questions: Am I harming my party? Am I in this for myself? Am I a total idiot who has no chance of winning? Three yeses and you're out. If each of the candidates takes this test tonight, tomorrow that party will have six candidates and a race worth watching.

On the Road

THERE WERE ONLY four of us on the road: myself, Don Spence, John Marshall and Michal Grajewski.

We called ourselves the Gentlemen of the Van. I can't remember why, or who came up with it. But it does sound like it could be a secret society of ten-year-olds that meets regularly in an abandoned van turned clubhouse deep in the woods. Considering the maturity of our many conversations, the name is appropriate.

Gentlemen of the Van was also the name of the text thread we were all included on. If any one of us wanted to message the entire group at once, with a question or an observation, we used that thread. The thread was deleted every single night, the concept of mutually assured destruction never far from our minds.

I have shared more laughs with these guys in the years we were on the road than anyone deserves. It's been a beautiful relationship. If that sounds a tad touchy-feely, like it's lifted from a magazine article entitled "Laugh every day: Tips for a healthy marriage," so be it. It is true. We laughed every day and we never went to bed angry—and the sex was nonexistent.

The *Mercer Report* never would have worked, or even survived, if not for this team.

There were weeks where we stood together next to three oceans within seven days. We have literally been to the tops of mountains and to the bottom of the sea together. We were together nonstop for long periods of time and never once came to blows. Show me a band that can say that.

Putting this road team together was Gerald's job.

Before we started the show, I had spent a lot of time travelling for *This Hour Has 22 Minutes.* I was good at being on the road, but it's all about who you travel with. The show we envisioned would mean even more time on the road and more time away from home.

For *Talking to Americans* and *This Hour Has 22 Minutes*, I travelled with cameraman Peter Sutherland and producer Geoff D'Eon. Both of them are incredible talents. I loved travelling with those guys, and the thought of doing a new show without them was daunting. But we had no choice. They lived in Nova Scotia. Moving to Toronto was not an option.

Gerald had only one choice for road director: John Marshall. They went way back. Before theatre school and then TV, Gerald was a bartender at an Ottawa bar called Studley's. John was the busboy. It was one of those bars whose claim to fame was that it had on display one of the actual tiles from the dance floor from *Saturday Night Fever.* No less than John Travolta had strutted here.

It was actually a piece of plexiglass from Canadian Tire with Christmas lights underneath it. Showbiz!

John's qualifications as producer and road director went far and beyond his ability to bus tables around drunks. After
Studley's he was, for a brief period of time, a messenger in the

office of Prime Minister Pierre Trudeau. For me, that alone was enough. But John had also studied broadcast journalism in Ottawa and spent the mid-eighties working at the epicentre of Canadian show business: *The Tommy Hunter Show*. Along the way he moved into comedy, producing shows with the likes of *SCTV*'s Andrea Martin, and *CODCO*'s Tommy Sexton and Greg Malone.

For nine years he produced *The New Music*—which put him on the road with George Stroumboulopoulos. He crossed the country with the Tragically Hip, went to Bangkok with Pearl Jam and London, England, with Moby. He has stories of shooting with Iggy Pop, Beyoncé, Joe Strummer and Green Day. He is a road warrior. Hiring John was the best call we ever made.

Don Spence, I believe, is the best cameraman in the country. Gerald and I worked with Don on a sitcom we produced called *Made in Canada*. He was our first choice for the new show, but he was a long shot. We were a new show and Don was then, as he is now, one of the most in-demand cameramen in the country.

I only ever heard one negative about Don. I was told by more than a few people that, while I was lucky to have him, eventually Don would get bored and move on to another show. Among our many achievements I am proudest of the fact that Don never got bored.

Why is Don so good? He is not a journeyman who just points and shoots. He is an artist. He can do it all because he has shot it all. He has shot drama, comedy, wildlife documentaries, World Cup downhill skiing, figure-skating specials, multiple Olympic events and countless Juno Awards shows. He has pointed his lens at everybody from Mr. Dressup to Nelson Mandela. His favourite thing in the world to shoot, other than me in thirty-below temperatures, is dance. Every time I see Veronica Tennant, she admonishes me for hiring him away from the dance world. It makes sense; to watch Don shoot is to watch him dance.

When the Tragically Hip's last concert was broadcast live to the nation, Don Spence was front and centre—his was Gord Downie's close-up camera. That is the definition of a go-to guy.

Rounding out the team was the "new guy"—associate road producer Michal Grajewski. He was with us for twelve of our fifteen years on the road. Mike's responsibilities are too many to list. He was the drone pilot, he set the GoPro cameras, he took all the photos on the road, he was the wheelman, he brought his brilliant improvising skills to every shoot. He could, without fail, make me laugh uncontrollably with his vocal impersonation of a certain deceased television personality—a routine so profoundly inappropriate we have promised never to speak of it in public. It's for the van only.

Mike's enthusiasm was always a great reminder to the rest of us of how lucky we were to be doing the show. He always found joy in every shoot. He would say, "Cool! They have rocks and they are labelled by age!" with the exact same exuberance as when he would say, "Cool! We're gonna fly in a fighter jet!" Every shoot was equally exciting. "This is going to be the best day ever!"

Mike is also known in certain hockey circles as "The Mayor of Little Winnipeg"—or at least that's what he has been called by *The New York Times*. A proud Winnipegger, when he's not at work he holds court during Winnipeg Jets games at a Toronto bar called Motel. Thanks in part to Mike's devotion to the team, the bar has become ground zero for Jets fans and displaced Winnipeggers alike in need of cold beer and Prairie hospitality.

Whether it's twelve years or fifteen, it is a very long time to be on the road with the same guys. That is a lot of 5 a.m. lobby calls and more than a few dodged moose and deer. Over that time you see everyone at their best and at their lowest. There is a bit of the "in sickness and in health, in good times and in bad" that goes on.

Don broke some ribs and didn't take a week off. I have broken a rib before—singular—and I found working excruciating. I should point out my job doesn't require heavy lifting. Don's requires lifting and running at the same time.

And Mike, it turns out, doesn't like heights. What a stupid job for someone who hates heights. And yet he persevered, setting a GoPro camera on the very tip of the tallest mast of the *Bluenose* schooner as it bobbed in the North Atlantic.

Recently I sent Mike a text asking him about the heights thing.

> Hey Mike, was setting the GoPro at the top of the mast of the Bluenose the scariest thing you had to do on the show?

> No. Are you crazy? It was scary, but that wasn't the scariest.

> C'mon, I don't think there were that many scary days.

> What about when we crashed in the hot air balloon?

> That was a crash. That doesn't count.

What about when we went up in the Harvard
airplane and the guy said we would burn to death
before we can land, so we have to jump at anything
above 500 feet WHICH IS NOT HIGH ENOUGH TO
JUMP AND LIVE!

He was exaggerating. And I was thinking about
heights.

Does hanging off the side of the World Financial
Centre in Shanghai without a harness count?

They have different regulations in that country,
different standards.

Well, I had to hang off the side of the Scotia Tower,
and I had to set a camera on the top of a telephone pole once, and remember we had to rappel
down the side of Mount Nimbus in BC? And what
about climbing the power line and then walking
out on the wires! And to the top of the mast on the
tall ship and I barfed all day and we didn't use the
shot? And what about when I crawled out the hole
on the side of the Confederation Bridge to PEI? Or
to the top of the Leviathan roller coaster at
Wonderland? Did I mention . . .

Okay, I think that's enough. But on the up side you
are over your fear of heights!

No, it's worse now.

Right. Okay—beers soon?

Yes please.

So Mike doesn't like heights.

I should also point out Mike doesn't like bees. And yet he persevered when he was placed among literally thousands of them, some crawling on his face as he set up his camera next to a massive bee colony.

Mike, as it turns out, does not want to be trampled by a herd of bison, yet he persevered when his job required him to stand with his back to a herd as they thundered around Elk Island National Park, Alberta.

There was a lot of perseverance.

Looking back, the amazing thing is that everyone showed up and worked no matter what, no matter their fear of snakes or heights or freezing water.

In fifteen years, John Marshall never missed a single day. He produced the hell out of any segment that was thrown at him, whether it was in a plane, under the water, on a mountain or in an unruly mob.

I say never missed a *day*, but he did miss *half* a day. It seems unfair that, after fifteen years of dedication to the process and a near-perfect track record, his singular lost afternoon should be talked about here, but . . . what the hell.

We were scheduled to shoot on a university campus in BC. Early in the morning Don and I found John near the hotel coffee machine and breakfast buffet. He wasn't getting coffee or food. He was just standing there, gazing into what I suppose could be called the middle distance. He looked awful.

Don and I exchanged glances. John is one of those people who looks exactly the same every time you see him. In fact, he looks exactly the same now as he did the day I met him twenty-five years ago. His idea of letting loose is having a second ginger ale. Whenever we agreed to meet in the lobby at six, the rest of us dragged ourselves down on time, but he was the one who had been in the pool at five. On this day he looked like he was the last man standing at the end of Burning Man.

"How you feeling?" I asked.

"I'm good," said John, "although I may have a little thing."

"You look awful," said Don.

Everything Don says is without alarm, in a nonchalant manner, and is the truth.

Me, I like to think I have a far more subtle bedside manner.

"You look a little flushed," I offered.

"You look like Jabba the Hutt," said Don.

"You are a little puffy," I agreed.

"No, I'm good," John said. "I feel fine. We should get going. If we have time I want to stop by a drugstore on the way. You guys should eat. We won't get lunch until middle of the afternoon."

Of course John wanted us to get going. It was his job to make sure the day ran on time and when it didn't, which was rare, it was his job to pivot and figure it out. He wasn't going to let his puffy face change that. The problem was, it wasn't just puffy, it was closing in on hideous.

As for the detour, we have all been on the planet long enough by now to know that when someone says they want to stop by the drugstore, you don't say, "Why? What do you need?" Some things are best left between a man and his pharmacist.

"Got to grab an EpiPen," he said.

"Oh my," said Don. "Really?"

"What the hell do you need an EpiPen for?" I asked.

"I might be having a reaction to some medication," he said

to nobody in particular. His eyes were not particularly focused at this point.

"Well, something is going on," said Don as if commenting on the weather. Don proceeded to scoop scrambled eggs from the chafing tray. "I'd get that looked at."

I have to admit, I was pretty worried at this point. If John's esophagus was swelling at the rate of his face, he was on borrowed time. I would have insisted that John stay at the hotel, but I knew he wouldn't agree to that. Also, seeing as we were tracking down an EpiPen, it was probably best if someone was with him when he fell to the ground, gasping for air.

Among the useful tips I have picked up on the road? EpiPens are available at any drugstore and they cost about a hundred bucks.

Turns out John was having an allergic reaction. John is allergic to penicillin, and because of that he hasn't touched the stuff since he was ten. However, his doctor informed him that times have changed and he prescribed a drug that was a "distant cousin" to penicillin, one he said was completely safe for John to take despite John's misgivings.

After said EpiPen was purchased we headed to the location, which thankfully was a relatively civilized shoot. John worked the phone in the van, confirming the interviews that he had scheduled, discussing elevator locations so we could transport the gear. I wasn't surprised. It is what he does, and he does it better than anyone.

While he continued doing everything he had to do as producer, I helped by reading aloud the instructions for the EpiPen.

"Apparently, I am to jam it as hard as I can into your thigh. John, do you have a preference?"

"Right thigh," said John. "Don't get my knee."

"Should I shoot that?" Don asked. "If it happens?"

"No, no," I said, although secretly I hoped he *would* film it because I would look heroic.

When we arrived at the location, things progressed as John had planned. He kept saying he was feeling fine, but I didn't believe him for a second. And at some point he started to look worse. I was of two minds about what to do. I knew he would not want to leave and go to a doctor—that because of some stupid show business dictate, he would see leaving us in mid-shoot as a dereliction of duty.

I decided I had to pull rank (an absurd notion, really, because there was no "rank" on the road). But someone had to do it because I knew John would not leave, no matter how fat his head got.

"John, you have to go to the hotel—or an emergency room. We will figure out a way to have someone keep an eye on you, but this is absurd. You have to get off your feet."

I knew he was feeling it now, because he said, "Okay, after you do this interview I'll go," and then he looked into the room where nine people had gathered, ready to be interviewed by me. "I'll just go in first and tell that guy he can't wear the fright wig if he wants to be in the shot."

One of the small production issues involved in this shoot was that it was taking place on Halloween. That meant that some people were in costume. This was not a big deal—things like this happen—but we were planning to run the piece in two weeks and we didn't want it to look dated, so we were doing everything we could to avoid showing students dressed as stormtroopers or Harry Potter.

I looked into the room to see who he was talking about. I did not see anyone in costume, and I did not see a man in a wig. I did, however, see a petite female professor whose hair, while perhaps alarming, was certainly her own and not a drugstore fright wig.

I reached for the EpiPen in my pocket. We could now add "completely delirious" to John's symptoms.

"I'll take care of the guy in the wig, John. Let's get you to a doctor."

An hour later, a doctor informed us John would live. John then went to sleep for seventeen hours and we flew home on Wednesday evening.

On Thursday he was back in the office, and by Friday he was in the alley directing that week's rant. He remained puffy for two weeks, after which he moulted like a snake and came out the other side looking as pretty as ever.

The EpiPen is now expired, having never been used.

Fifteen years. We all lived happily ever after.

John and me in Prime Minister Trudeau's office. On his desk are small cue cards with each province and the name of the premier. He has to know all that stuff!

Not sure where this crew picture was taken. Perhaps the West Edmonton Mall?

So you want me to crawl up a transmission tower and then sit on the wires? Sure, what could go wrong?

HIRE SOME CANADIANS

February 28, 2017

I have followed politics in this country my entire life. I have seen governments come and I have seen governments go. And I've noticed they've all got a few things in common. One: I believe they all try their best. Two: No matter how hard they try, they cannot build or buy ships. What governments *can* do is announce they're building ships and then later cancel the ships.

Building ships is one of the most complicated things in the entire world. The numbers alone are astronomical. We're talking billions and billions of dollars. And no matter what the agreed-upon cost, there is always a clause that says if anyone breaks wind, the price goes up 200 percent.

Luckily for governments, most people would never question anything about ship procurement because they just don't feel smart enough. I get this. I mean, who am I to say anything about the building of an icebreaker or a warship. But some things I do understand. For example, I know that the government of Canada is paying Irving Shipbuilding in Nova Scotia thirty billion dollars to build ships. And they have created lots of high-skill jobs.

But the slippery slope of job loss is beginning. Irving has closed its carpentry shop and it's now bringing in carpenters from Spain. Carpenters. I don't know much, but I know this: We've got carpenters. Alberta's got carpenters. I would go so far as to suggest that Alberta might even have some carpenters who are looking for work.

Look, I get it. If you have a project and you need a specialty act—like, you need someone who knows how to land the satellite on the comet—by all means bring in Dr. Gillibonky and his team. But if Irving needs people to install wall panelling, which is what those carpenters are doing, hire Canadian or give the thirty billion back.

TRUMP CARD

February 7, 2017

L iberal prime ministers always prefer it when a Democrat is president of the United States. Just look at the very special relationship that existed between Barack Obama and Justin Trudeau. Well, actually, those guys were a little over the top. I mean, Justin was barely elected for five minutes before he was having sleepovers at the White House. They're like people who meet on Tinder and decide to get married inside of a week. So when Donald Trump was elected, a lot of the experts said, yes, this could be bad for Canada, but this is definitely going to be very, very bad for Justin Trudeau.

Look, we all accept it: living next to the United States is like sleeping with an elephant. But suddenly the elephant has rabies and he's acting like someone is stabbing him in the eye with a fork. But for Trudeau, this could be a blessing. Thanks to Donald Trump, the Prime Minister can now get away with anything. He's totally off the radar. Just last week Justin Trudeau broke a major campaign promise on electoral reform. Inside the bubble of Ottawa, people lost it. The NDP called him a liar. Elizabeth May started sobbing. An entire generation of young first-time voters who voted Liberal because of that promise were gutted. And the rest of the country said, "Holy heck, Harold—look what Donald Trump is doing."

Our government is supposed to release a budget any day now. There's a rumour out there that our deficit has ballooned to three times the original estimate. That kind of thing could normally prove fatal for a government. But if, on that day, Donald Trump wakes up and opens his mouth—or, God forbid, updates his Twitter feed—the chance of anyone paying any attention to anything to do with numbers is very slim.

Donald Trump is like a natural disaster, except one that reoccurs every day. That is good luck for Justin Trudeau for as long as it lasts. And if the last eighteen days are any indication, he's got about four years of good luck left.

THE FACTS ARE OUT

January 31, 2017

For the past decade not a day has gone by when I have not reflected on how truly amazing the internet is. Multiple times a day I've wondered how we ever survived before smart phones.

Just imagine if someone from the old days—say the seventies or eighties—time-travelled to 2017. Their minds would be blown at the amount of knowledge that we all carry around in our cell phones. But what would they think when we told them, "Oh, half the information is false." And not just false, but intentionally false, designed to confuse us. Fake news. "Cancer is a conspiracy"; "oil of oregano will cure meningitis"; "the climate is not changing". All headlines, all fake.

Not that long ago, if you were in business or politics and you were caught intentionally spreading lies about an opponent, it would be game over. You would be out. You would be considered a dishonourable human being. Now it's everywhere.

Here in Canada we have the very successful Dr. Kellie Leitch leadership campaign. Running for leadership of the Conservative party. Her campaign manager brags that he spreads false news on her behalf. The consequences? Nothing. I would love to see Dr. Leitch and her manager in a town hall—except a town hall full of children—and watch the good doctor try to explain to the kids why lying is okay.

Of course it's not lying anymore, is it? It's just spreading "alternative facts." I have searched the internet high and low. There is one question for which I cannot find the answer: Why is it that now, when we have access to more information than ever before, we are becoming increasingly dumb?

CANADA–US RELATIONS: TBD

January 24, 2017

ecently when I was poking around on Wikipedia, I found myself browsing through a series of bizarre medical conditions. Anything to avoid reading about Kevin O'Leary. Anyway, one of them was this very rare psychiatric condition called Capgras syndrome. With Capgras, a person wakes up one morning and is suddenly convinced that people they are very familiar with—people they love—have been replaced by identical, unpredictable replicants. And I thought, "Gosh, what a terrible thing." But then I thought, "Hey, that's exactly how I feel about the United States since Election Day." It's like the entire country has been replaced by aliens. Or at least 47 percent of them. It's the only plausible explanation.

So, what does a Trump presidency mean? I have no idea, but I know that as of now, the phrase "stranger things have happened" has been upgraded from expression to absolute truth. If tomorrow morning I am shaving and I sneeze and a little bird pops out of my nose and chirps "O Canada," I will think, "That's strange. Not as strange as what's happening south of the border, but it's up there."

And what does President Trump mean for Canada? From a diplomatic point of view, we must proceed with caution. I call it the 3 a.m. protocol. It's 3 a.m., the bars have closed and you're walking down the street. Suddenly some big guy is coming right at you. All you can do is keep your head up, avoid eye contact, walk with purpose and get ready to run like hell. Because that glassy-eyed giant mumbling incoherently is capable of anything. He could just be coming for a great big hug, maybe he wants directions to a pizza place, or maybe he's gonna stick you with a shiv.

45

Welcome to a new chapter in Canada–US relations. Here's hoping it will be a mutually beneficial relationship. Stranger things have happened.

AGA KHAN, AGA CAN'T

January 17, 2017

Fourteen months ago, Canadians were up to our necks in a federal election. And in hindsight, the Liberal campaign was a force to behold. There were no missteps. And when it came to public opinion, the Liberals knew exactly what would not pass the smell test. Now the campaign is over, they've suddenly lost their sense of smell and are losing their sense of balance.

Hey Justin, what's the definition of amazing? Amazing is being prime minister of Canada. Best job ever, and let's face it, some great perks. But like all public servants, there are sacrifices. For example, if an old family friend—say, I don't know, the Aga Khan—calls up and says, "Hey Justin! What say you, the wife and your family come on down to my private island for the holidays?" You've got to say no. "No, I'm sorry, Aga. I would love to come down and put on a gold hat and lie by the pool with you and Tattoo, but I can't. I can't because my government gives your foundation millions of dollars a year, so I've got to take a rain cheque."

I know, Justin, this is unfair. After all, my father worked

with a fellow named Jerry. Jerry's got a cabin on the Gander River and he's thrown me the keys a few times. There's no helicopter, but there's a lovely view and a cupboard filled with free coffee whitener. I hope to go back someday. I probably will. Canadians have always bummed cabins and cottages. In fact, it's part of our heritage. I'm sorry you can't do the same, Justin, but that's just the cost of doing business. And your business is being prime minister of Canada. First, foremost and only. Focus on that. If you don't, it won't matter. You'll be back on Fantasy Island in no time.

HASHTAGS AND THE DAMAGE DONE
December 6, 2016

Here we are, in the first week of December, and dare I say, it's beginning to feel a lot like Christmas. Not because of the sights or sounds of the season, but because my Facebook feed is beginning to fill up with pictures of people's Christmas trees. And boy, there are some nice trees out there. I swear some people do a Google image search of "best tree ever" and then post it as their own. It's times like this I'm convinced that Facebook and Instagram were invented to make people feel like they're failing at their own lives—or at the very least, failing at the holidays.

I have a friend who takes Christmas very seriously. She works 24/7, weeks and months in advance. The entire extended family shows up, but it's worth it. On Facebook she looks like Martha Stewart. Every picture is stunningly beautiful—#Christmas! #Family! #Peace! Meanwhile, in real life, she's like, "See that picture of all of us smiling around the tree? Thirty minutes later the yelling started. Then the baby threw the green peas—scattered from one end of the house to the other." By the time the holidays are over, Mom is *this* close to being institutionalized. But she's one of the lucky ones; she's still surrounded by people. She actually loves three-quarters of those in attendance.

Christmas is very hard on a lot of people. There's a lot to live up to and people fall through the cracks. It's lonely out there, plus it gets dark at 5 p.m. This year, let's not aim for perfect; let's aim for lovely. Let's count our blessings, take a moment and make it easier for someone else.

THE PROBLEM WITH CARDING
November 29, 2016

It's happening all over the country and it has for years. Saskatoon, Edmonton, Toronto, Halifax—the list goes on. It's called "carding." Well, the kids call it "carding"; the police call it "street checks." This is the practice, used by some police forces, of randomly stopping citizens on the street and questioning them. You know: Who are you? Where are you going? Who do you know? What's your height? What's your weight? Do you have tattoos? It's all documented, including perceived skin colour. Which is why we know that young black men are carded disproportionately more than anyone else.

White people are carded too. I'm sure I've seen it happen. Or was that an old war movie where the officer demanded, "May I see your papers, please?" for no reason whatsoever.

Carding has always been controversial, but instead of just scrapping it, they just keep changing the rules to make it more palatable. For example, in Toronto, starting on New Year's Day, they will continue to card but will no longer card anyone based on their race. Wow, there are baby steps and then there are little, tiny baby steps.

This is a tough one for me. I have complete respect for police officers and the job they do. In this country, people call the cops for everything—from every bump in the night to every serious crime, to a million things in between. It is go, go, go with that job. Where they find the time to card people, I have no idea. But it happens too often.

I have never been stopped and questioned by the police for no reason. I have never felt intimidated. I hate to think that is in part because of the colour of my skin. I like cops. I like to see cops coming. If we stop carding, maybe eventually everyone will feel the same, regardless of race.

People are finally starting to pay attention to the Conservative leadership race. Normally, that would make me so happy. I just wish they were paying attention, because there are thirteen candidates, from all walks of life, from all regions of Canada, with very exciting ideas.

Not so much.

People are mostly paying attention because Dr. Kellie Leitch has emerged as a frontrunner. You remember her. During the last election, she was the one who wanted to introduce a "barbaric cultural practices" hotline to Canada. Sort of like a toll-free number you could call if brown people moved into your neighbourhood. That policy cost the Tories the election, but it launched her leadership bid.

She is a very impressive candidate. She's trilingual—she speaks English, French and a secret language that only really angry white people can understand. Her latest plan is that all visitors to this country must be screened for "Canadian values." No biggie, really—if you look like me and your cousins show up from California or the UK, you'll be fine; if your name is Omar or Ahmed, you might want to schedule a few extra hours out at the airport. Or maybe you could go visit *them.*

A lot of Conservatives say we should just ignore her because she's just doing this to get attention. I don't buy that. There are far less offensive ways to get attention. I got on the subway the other day and a dude had a tattoo of an excited pig on his face. Certainly got my attention. I wouldn't vote for the guy but who knows, maybe some people would. In a post-Trump world, anything is possible.

Look, leader of the Conservative party is a very big job. It is just steps away from the prime minister's office. And in 150 years, no one has made it there simply by race-baiting. If you're a Conservative, please get involved; otherwise, someone might.

A DANGEROUS EXPERIMENT
November 15, 2016

Eight years ago, on November 4, I was lucky enough to find myself in New York City. It was the night that Barack Obama was first elected president of the United States of America. History in the making. The feeling of optimism and "yes we can" was on bust. And I remember thinking, "In my entire life, I will never again witness an election as transformative as this one." And I also remember thinking, "Tonight, America deserves the title 'greatest nation on Earth.'"

Eight years later, it turns out I was wrong on both fronts. Who would have guessed that after electing a black president twice, they would follow up with an orange one?

It turns out it's true that in America, anyone can grow up to be president. Narcissist? Tax dodger? Do your hobbies include sitting around on a giant gold throne? Yes? By all means, please advance to the front of the line.

Our neighbours to the south have made a choice. Some suggest this choice was made out of anger. To the angry

American voter, I say, "Next time, why not punch a wall or go for a walk around the block?" Because this is a very dangerous experiment you have embarked on. Obviously we honour your choice. And as Canadians, your greatest friends and admirers, we will welcome Chachi as the new US ambassador. And as far as the new president goes, let's hope that moving forward the magnitude and dignity of the office wins the day.

PARTLY CLOUDY SUNNY WAYS

November 1, 2016

One year and a bit ago, Justin Trudeau won his majority government. Sunny ways, my friends, sunny ways. And on this "Trudeauversary" two stories caught my eye. The first one is about the fundraising. Thanks to Justin Trudeau, any average Canadian citizen with a dream and fifteen hundred dollars can go to a party, eat cheese and get one-on-one time with a cabinet minister. Now, this kind of thing has gone on since 1867. The difference is, Justin Trudeau promised straight up it would never happen on his watch.

It's called "cash for access." And that's what it's all about: access. Why else would anyone pay any money at all to see the finance minister in person? It's not like the man can sing. "Honey—good news! I just scored two tickets to see

Bill Morneau in some rich dude's living room. Only cost us three grand for the pair," said no person ever.

The other story involved Justin himself. Off he went to the Canadian Labour Congress to speak to a youth forum, and the youth, they booed him. Wow, that's got to hurt. I don't remember Stephen Harper ever being booed at an oil-and-gas conference.

And what did Justin Trudeau say to these angry young people who were upset because he's not fulfilling his promises? Justin said he was the one who was "disappointed" in *them*. Yes, he used the word *disappointed*. He really is a teacher, isn't he? If I had a dollar for every time a teacher told me they were disappointed with me, well, I guess I could buy a ticket to drink bad wine and hang out with the finance minister.

Sunny ways, my friend, sunny ways. One year out. They're starting to lose their way.

OUT OF LINE

October 25, 2016

It has been suggested, on occasion, that I lack patience. So I decided to devote the necessary time to improve myself. And after spending five minutes this morning in a Tim Hortons, I realized I don't lack patience at all. My problem is I live in a city, as do the vast majority of Canadians.

My problem is I share my city with a tiny minority of people who are completely oblivious to anyone else around them. And by "around them," I mean they don't care about anyone behind them in a lineup.

You cannot avoid lineups in a big city. But how is it that there are people who walk among us who do not understand that when you're in a lineup, you're supposed to figure out what you want to order before you get to the counter? It's a coffee shop; you know what you drink, order it. You're not choosing your university major.

Inevitably these people are the "exact change" people. You know who they are. It comes to $1.75, they've got a toonie, but they don't want to use the toonie. They want to pay with exact change. The hell with everyone behind them in the lineup; all they've got to do to pay is stop everything, bend over, pick up their purse or their backpack, put it on the counter, open the zipper, reach inside, root around—no, no, wrong compartment. Close that zipper, open the next one—reach in, got it, got it . . . oh no, hang on, it's another smaller purse or wallet with lots of little compartments, one of which is for the nickel. They find the nickels slowly, slowly count out the nickels—not enough nickels. Hang on, they've got a quarter somewhere else. And these people, they always look back and smile at the rest of us in the line as if we're enjoying this as much as they are.

People of the city, we are in this together. Yes, patience is a virtue, and so is not acting like you're the only person on the planet. If you find yourself at the front of the line, keep it moving, because tomorrow, guaranteed, you'll be at the back.

BLAME THE ELITES

October 18, 2016

The problem with this country, in a nutshell, is the elites. This problem has nothing to do with money; it is all about attitude. And another thing: The elites are not just a menace, they are the last group of people in society you can attack and get away with it. And it works.

Look at Kellie Leitch. She is now the frontrunner for the leadership of the Conservative Party of Canada, in part because she has the courage to attack the elites. Not just the elites in the Liberals and the NDP and under her bed, but the elites in her own party. Apparently, they are everywhere. It's a good strategy. If history has taught us anything, it's that certain political movements do very well when they can blame all of life's problems on an identifiable group. And in the old days you could just pick a minority and have at 'em. You can't do that anymore. If you just start attacking willy-nilly the Jews, the gays, the people in wheelchairs, even people with university degrees, they will stand up. They will fight back.

Nobody identifies as an elite, so no one will fight back. Nobody wants to wear that. I have been called every name in the book; I really don't care. If someone called me elite, I'd be all defensive. I'd be like, "You can't call me elite. I grew up with a goat as a lawn mower. I was taught that good manners means you don't slurp when you're drinking the juice out of the tin of Vienna sausages."

So no more. If you hear someone blaming the elites, you just swap out that word for whatever group you're a member of. That's all you need to know. Calling someone an elite is nothing but an empty insult from an empty mind.

OUR WATER ISN'T FREE

Recently a small township in Ontario by the name of Centre Wellington tried to buy a well. Because as a growing municipality it wanted access to clean, safe drinking water into the future. Why anyone would be worried about such a thing, I have no idea, but hey, it's a free country. Anyway, long story short, it didn't work out. The township didn't get its well. It didn't get its well because it was outbid by Nestlé, a giant multinational. And now Nestlé can suck all the water it wants out of that well and put it in little plastic bottles and sell it to people who need the water in order to live.

Let's be clear: companies like Nestlé can't just take water for free. No, this is a great natural resource, one that belongs to we, the people. Companies have to pay for the privilege. How much do they pay? Well, they pay three dollars and seventy-one cents for every million litres of water they take. I'm just going to repeat that because you might be thinking, "Well, that can't be right." They pay three dollars and seventy-one cents for every million litres of water they take.

The amount of water these companies suck out of Canada is staggering. We are talking trillions of litres of water every single day. These are numbers you can't even begin to get your head around unless you're on the spectrum.

Canada is one of the greatest countries on Earth. We have one-fifth of the world's freshwater supply. Every Canadian should have access to clean water out of a tap or a hose. But the multinationals? They should pay through the nose. Let's tell Nestlé and the entire industry that we may be a free country, but our water is not.

ILL WIND FROM THE SOUTH

October 4, 2016

A t this point there have been millions of articles written about the US presidential election. My guess is that half of them include the phrase "reality TV," and I understand the comparison. But in order for a reality TV show to work, it has to be, at its core, fundamentally vulgar. Or as it's referred to now, Trump-like.

The US election is not reality TV. The great thing about reality TV is if you don't want to watch, you don't have to watch. Believe it or not, there are people among us who can't pick a Kardashian out of a police lineup. At least from the front. But we can't just decide to not watch a US election. In fact, as Canadians we should pay very, very close attention. Not so we can feel superior, but as a cautionary tale.

In Canada we have three major political parties; two of those parties have no leaders. The fact that Donald Trump is the Republican nominee in the States will have a huge impact on those races right here in Canada. Look at the NDP. The party of Douglas. The party of Layton. Nobody even wants the job. They are just sitting there, waiting for a hostile takeover. Literally, someone shows up with a few bucks, a name and the will to live? The party could be theirs.

And the Tories? Well, the opposite is true. They could have well over a dozen people on stage for their first leadership debate. The Republicans had sixteen. What happened? The outrageous one, the one that played the race card and the fear card, Donald Trump, was the last one standing. And it's pretty obvious that some Tories up here have been paying very close attention to that strategy.

So, to the membership of the NDP and the Conservatives: When choosing your leaders, remember it is an ill wind that blows from the south. What happened down there can happen here. Don't let it.

UNBELIEVABLE

March 29, 2016

When I read the story of Felipe Montoya in *The Globe and Mail*, I knew that something was not right. It wasn't a big story. It was, in fact, a small story. It was a page-five story, and yet it did not pass the smell test.

Felipe came to Canada four years ago from Costa Rica with his wife and two kids. The man is highly educated. He is now a full-time, tenured professor at York University. He's got a big job. He pays taxes. The perfect citizen.

But this is where the story becomes hard to believe. According to *The Globe and Mail*, the government of Canada has said Felipe and his family cannot stay in Canada; they cannot become permanent residents because his son has Down syndrome. Okay, this is where I thought the story cannot be true. I mean, I know Canada is not perfect, but surely to God we are not throwing children out of the country because they have Down syndrome.

Well, apparently, that is exactly what we are doing. Apparently, there is a war on kids with Down syndrome that I was completely unaware of. The government's position is that because the kid has Down syndrome, he could potentially become a burden on the system.

Really? We're going to predict that now? What's next? We're gonna say that a family can't come in because that kid in grade eight just failed his math test or that one's got a funny foot?

There are absolutely no guarantees in this life when it comes to predicting who will contribute what to society. Some dude with Down syndrome working at Loblaws contributes a hell of a lot more than some of the guys I went to high school with— people I am proud to call my friends and fellow Canadians.

I was so hoping this story was untrue. I was wrong. Here's hoping that our new government, with its sunny ways, sees the error of its ways.

My Canada includes an extra chromosome.

TIME FOR TOM TO GO
March 22, 2016

In just three weeks, members of the New Democratic Party of Canada, or the NDP, will be gathering in Edmonton for their annual policy convention. Now, I know what a lot of you are thinking. You're thinking, "Who are the NDP again? Why is that name so familiar?" Well, back in the olden days, like ten months ago, they were the party that was going to win the federal election. Their leader, Tom Mulcair, was ahead in the polls. Confidence was high. Team Mulcair was in it to win it. We don't need to dwell on what happened next.

Okay, let's dwell.

The NDP came in third; Justin Trudeau became prime minister; Stephen Harper resigned to spend more time with his anger. But Tom Mulcair, he stayed on the job. Why he wants this job, I have no idea. Although I have seen this type of behaviour before. There was a dude in Iowa who won the lotto and still went to work the next day, cleaning out sewers. So there is a precedent.

But if Tom stays on as leader, he's got to go to this convention, and he's got to stand there while the members vote on whether they want to keep him or not. If 50 percent plus one say he's got to go, he's got to go. And anything less than a 70 percent approval rating is kind of embarrassing.

Tom, you were a great leader of the opposition. Perhaps the best one Canada has ever seen. So you didn't become prime minister, big deal. That's a very big club—there's like thirty-six million people in that club. If you leave now, you can escape with your pension and your dignity. Very few people get out of politics with both. You stick around, and your own party may take away the latter. Life is unfair. Politics is worse.

DARKEST HOUR

March 15, 2016

This past Sunday the clocks jumped ahead an hour. We all lost an hour of sleep. Daylight saving time is now in effect. It happens every year at this time. We don't question it, we just change the clocks. And so, the day after, I'm walking around, I'm in a bad mood because I didn't get enough sleep, and I'm mumbling to myself that daylight saving time is stupid. I admit this was not based on any evidence; this was just me being grumpy.

But then I did something that's very dangerous: I Googled. Turns out there is a group of like-minded geniuses out there who have the exact same opinion as I do. They believe daylight saving time is very bad idea for a bunch of reasons, the least of which is that it drives children berserk. True thing. Also, in the forty-eight hours after the clocks go ahead, men keel over in droves with heart attacks. Not that men need a lot of excuses to have heart attacks, but still the data is very troubling.

Car accidents go through the roof, which makes perfect sense. The Monday after the clocks go ahead, the roads are suddenly filled with people who are late for work, in a bad mood and half-asleep. Call this what it is. It's not daylight saving time—it's a population cull. And it should stop now.

And in the fall, when the clocks go back, that's even deadlier—though we do gain an hour of sleep, so that one I can live with.

MARS, HERE I COME

March 8, 2016

I am at a complete and utter loss as to what is happening in the United States. I can't even begin to understand what is happening to the Republican Party. How is it that the party of Eisenhower, the party of Abraham Lincoln, has become the plaything for the owner of the Miss Universe beauty pageant? And how is it possible that the more outrageous Donald Trump becomes, the higher his approval ratings go? I don't get it.

At this point, I wouldn't be surprised if he chose Honey Boo Boo as his running mate.

But what's truly disturbing is that we in Canada are not immune to this behaviour. Ten days ago Conservatives from all over Canada gathered in Ottawa for the Manning Conference. There was one subject on their mind: who would be the next leader of the Conservative Party of Canada. And who got all the attention? Who was the big star? Kevin O'Leary from *Dragons' Den*. A man whose entire shtick is that money is a religion. And the more outrageous he became, the more they loved him. It's embarrassing. He's up here in Canada doing Donald Trump's act—not as well—and it's working. He's like a Rod Stewart impersonator. Big crowds in small towns only.

But thanks to Kevin O'Leary, I now relate to those Americans who say that if Trump becomes president, they want to move to Canada. Because if Trump becomes president and Kevin O'Leary becomes prime minister, I want to leave the planet. Seriously, I would rather live in a bubble on Mars and eat potatoes grown in my own poo. Trump and O'Leary? Stop the world, I want to get off.

PR OPPORTUNITY

March 1, 2016

Ever since I've been following politics, ever since I was a kid, there were always people around who loved to talk about proportional representation—or as they like to call it, PR. Which means changing our democratic system entirely.

Basically, it means taking what we've got now, throwing it out and changing it so that the number of seats a political party has in the House of Commons reflects the percentage of the vote the party received. All you have to know is that it's the Green Party's all-time favourite fantasy.

I never spent much time thinking about this PR business because, quite frankly, it was always academic. It was the domain of political nerds. I figured if it's never going to happen in my lifetime, why should I even think about it? Kind of the way I used to feel about a Justin Trudeau majority.

But recently, something astounding happened.

There's an organization devoted to making PR happen. It's called Every Voter Counts. Until just days ago, and don't take this the wrong way, this alliance was made up of the usual gang of lefty suspects: the Broadbent Institute, Idle No More, the Canadian Labour Congress. All good people, all firmly on the left.

But now Stephen Harper's former chief of staff, Guy Giorno—a giant in Conservative circles—has joined the gang.

Just to be clear, Stephen Harper's chief of staff sitting down with the Ed Broadbent people is kind of like Darth Vader sitting down with the Ewoks to fight climate change.

I don't know what this means, but I kind of like it. Smart people, political rivals, coming together with one goal: improve our democracy. These are very interesting times indeed. It may be the worst of times for our economy, but the best of times for Canada.

SMUGNESS RESTORED

February 9, 2016

So the other night I get home from work and it's a few minutes before *The National*. I'm flicking around and up pops Anderson Cooper reviewing the day's events on the American campaign trail, and I'm hooked. Trump versus Cruz. Hillary versus Bernie. Cruz. Trump. Did I mention Trump? I could not avert my eyes.

I felt a little guilty because, let's face it, I was not watching because I have an innate interest in the American political process. I was watching because, well, it's a train wreck down there. Actually, that's too kind. The American primaries are like a train wreck in a trailer park and a tornado is coming. Plus, there are killer bees.

So in other words, the natural order of things has been restored. Canadian society functions at its best when we can collectively look down our noses on American politics with a certain smugness. We are happiest when we can look at each other and go, "That would never, ever happen up here." See, I miss that feeling.

For years it didn't matter where you were on the planet; mentioning that you were from Canada would open a ten-minute conversation about Mayor Ford, who they believed was the president or the king of Canada. But it didn't matter. That was our brand.

And the Americans had Obama and we had—well, let's not reflect on what we had. Let's celebrate what Canada has right now—boring mayors and a prime minister who has yet to say something completely insane. I know, it's shallow, but it feels good in the short term.

So thank you, America. You have nine months until Election Day. We will be watching for all the wrong reasons.

The Norman Jewison Affair

THEY SAY IT'S GOOD TO spend time around young people because their energy and enthusiasm is infectious. Perhaps. But it has been my experience that if you want either energy or enthusiasm, you should spend some time with Norman Jewison.

For anyone who is unaware, Norman Jewison is a very big deal in the world of cinema.

He has won the Irving G. Thalberg Memorial Award, which is the highest honour that can be given by the Academy of Motion Picture Arts and Sciences and is presented during the Oscar broadcast. Other recipients include Alfred Hitchcock, Walt Disney, Cecil B. DeMille, Steven Spielberg and Ingmar Bergman. Good company.

Norman's movies have won a boatload of Oscars. He has worked with the biggest stars in Hollywood and has done so for over six decades. He made *In the Heat of the Night*, *The Hurricane*, *Fiddler on the Roof*, *The Thomas Crown Affair*, *Jesus Christ Superstar* and many more . . . it's an embarrassment of cinematic riches.

That said, he appeared on the *Mercer Report* in 2011 not in his capacity as a filmmaker, but as one of the people who, in the early eighties, saved Christmas. Or at least Canada's largest Santa Claus parade.

The Toronto event was, from its inception, known to everyone as the Eaton's Santa Claus Parade. It was by far the largest of its kind in North America. Long story short, the Eaton family, owners of the legendary Canadian department store chain, woke up one morning and realized they had forgotten to mind the shop. The company was on the verge of collapse. Sponsorship of the parade was one of the first things to go.

It was Norman and a group of Toronto businesspeople, including Paul Godfrey, Ron Barbaro and George Cohon, who stepped forward and found a way to save the parade. The parade's continued survival is due in great part to their efforts.

One way they came up with for raising money was to offer people with deep pockets the opportunity to appear in the parade as "celebrity clowns." To this day more than 150 celebrity clowns march the parade's route at the beginning of each year's extravaganza. It is a significant fund-raiser. And in return for their sizable donations these clowns get sore feet and thousands of smiles.

Norman appeared on the *Mercer Report* and gave me tips on how to be a parade clown. A part he has played many times.

How many children over the years were given candy or a tissue for their runny nose by the director of *Moonstruck*? Nobody knows. Certainly not the kids. Norman always appears anonymously. Like all the clowns in Toronto's parade, celebrities or otherwise. Big wigs, red noses, painted faces. The epitome of dignity in public service in floppy shoes.

It was my great privilege not so long ago to deliver a toast to Norman on the occasion of his ninetieth birthday at the

Canadian Film Centre. A centre which he himself founded. I should mention that, while I was honoured to MC the event along with comedy legend Eugene Levy, I went to Norman's birthday party against the wishes of my mother, who thinks Norman is a bad influence on me. More about that later.

Norman made one of my favourite movies of all time: *The Russians Are Coming, the Russians Are Coming.*

The movie is legendary—it's one of the great satires. Made at the height of the Cold War, it was about a Russian submarine that goes off course and gets stuck on a sandbar next to a small town on the Eastern Seaboard of the United States. The hapless Russians in the grounded sub are terrified they will be captured and shot. Their only chance at survival is to sneak into town to get supplies to fix their submarine.

When the Americans living in this picturesque resort realize that there are Russians in their midst, Cold War hysteria breaks out. The townsfolk are convinced that the United States is being invaded, and they alone are the only line of defence against the communist superpower.

The film was brilliant. How brilliant? After it was released John Wayne threatened to beat the shit out of Norman at a Hollywood party—because clearly he was a Canadian commie. Now that's hitting a nerve.

So I knew Norman was a great film director. What I didn't know was that on occasion he watches TV.

Because one day in 2014, out of the blue, I got a phone call from Norman Jewison asking me if I would work on a script with him for a remake of—*The Russians Are Coming, the Russians Are Coming.* To this day, that phone call remains one of the most absurd and fantastic experiences of my life.

And while I sat with the phone to my ear and my jaw on

the ground, Norman told me how he saw this reboot—that instead of hapless Russians on a submarine, it would be hapless Iraqi circus performers who take a wrong turn and end up in the wrong town, where they are mistaken for a terrorist cell hell-bent on destroying America.

He was a little ahead of his time.

I had no idea whether it would work or not, but I said yes. If Norman had called me up and asked me to wash his car, I would have responded by asking if he wanted it waxed as well.

Days later, I met Norman at his office and we began what has become a wonderful friendship.

Just entering the office was a real thrill. It is a Hollywood time capsule. Norman bought the building in downtown Toronto many decades ago, and his office sits on the top floor. It's the ultimate sixties man cave. If Austin Powers made pictures, this is where he would hang. It's got shag carpet, and dimmer switches are built into the vintage coffee and end tables. There are director's chairs, giant art deco ashtrays and signed pictures of everyone from Doris Day to Frank Sinatra.

Every day I would meet Norman at his office and we would work on this movie script. For me, it was a master class. When he punched the clock there was no idle chitchat. It was all business. Plot, structure, character development. There was only one subject: the project at hand. He was a machine.

But at lunch? Or on a break? Then he was a font of showbiz stories. I would look up on the wall and see a picture of Norman with Dean Martin and ask, "What was Dean Martin like?" And of course there would be a great story. He met Dean while directing Judy Garland's first TV special.

Think of a legend, and Norman had a story. Karl Malden, Edward G. Robinson, Denzel Washington, Faye Dunaway,

Olympia Dukakis, Michael Caine, Tony Curtis—he worked with them all. His next-door neighbour in Malibu was Don Rickles. How could there not be stories?

We got along fabulously. The age gap of forty-plus years presented no problems at all. Except for one.

My phone.

I check my phone. I check my phone a lot. Sometimes I check my phone and I don't even realize I am checking it—it's not just my phone, it's my fidget spinner. Maybe I am addicted—at least I have the strength to admit it.

Norman hates the phone.

"Why are you looking at your phone?" he'd say. "We're working here."

"Right," I would say, putting it back down, but never putting it away.

Finally, one day, he let me have it.

"In my day when you were making a picture, you would work in a bungalow on a Hollywood lot. You would come into the office in the morning and you would say, 'Hold my calls,' and they held your calls. The way people knew you were working was they couldn't get a hold of you. And you got work done because you weren't wasting time talking on the phone. Your generation, you look at your phone every time the bloody thing beeps, and it's never important—half the time, as far as I can tell, it's someone you know sending you a picture of the salad they had for lunch."

He had a point. I've received my fair share of salad pics.

So I made a decision. A very difficult decision. I put the phone away . . . for Norman.

"Norman, you are right. I am sorry. I am here to work. You'll never see my phone again." I put it away.

Norman said, "I don't believe it."

We went back to work. And true to my word, the phone never saw the light of day again. At least not in front of him.

About a week later, we were at work when I got up from the table and headed for the washroom. Norman told me that the regular washroom in the main office was acting up, so it was best that I use the small one in the inner office—"First door on your right."

I headed to the room, an area of the office I had never been in before. I found the door and sure enough, there was a small half bath, sink and toilet.

I was standing there, having a leak and minding my own business, when I saw that above the toilet was a framed black-and-white picture. It showed a young Norman Jewison directing a young and very handsome Steve McQueen in *The Cincinnati Kid*.

They were on set in the pouring rain, and Steve McQueen was lying on the ground, back propped up against a wall, in a white shirt that's pasted to his body. Norman was leaning over and giving him direction.

For perhaps the hundredth time that month, I was amazed to think where I was. "I'm really here working with Jewison. Look at the legends this guy has worked with. Steve McQueen—at the time, he was the biggest actor of his day. He was a giant sex symbol. *The Cincinnati Kid* was a huge film."

It dawned on me that my mother would get a huge kick out of this photograph. She, like every woman of the era, loved Steve McQueen. So I took my phone out of my pocket and took a picture of the picture on the wall.

I walked back to the main office and sent a fast email to my mother. I typed, "Look who's hanging out with Steve McQueen today," and attached the picture, just as I was rounding the corner to the main office.

Norman was waiting for me outside the door. "I knew you were in there checking your phone," he said, quite pleased with himself.

I hit send, shoved the phone into my pocket and went back to work.

That night, after I had been home a few hours, I realized I hadn't heard anything from my mother. I called her and said, "Did you get the picture I sent you?"

She said, "Yes—and I didn't think much of it." Then she quickly hung up on me.

My initial thought was that I'd taken a picture of a picture in bad lighting—the bloody thing probably didn't turn out. It must've been a blur.

So I forwarded the picture to my laptop, opened it up and took a look.

The picture I took while taking a leak had turned out perfectly. You could tell who it was, all right.

The email was titled, "Look who's hanging out with Steve McQueen today." And attached was a picture of Steve McQueen and Norman Jewison. And framed perfectly between the two of them, reflected in the glass, was my penis.

Thanks to this Hollywood legend and his aversion to cell phones, I had sent my mother a dick pic.

A bad influence indeed.

I told that story at his ninetieth birthday party. I look forward to hearing his version of events at mine.

John and me in the House of Commons. We are discussing lunch.

(above) *Sometimes it was necessary to go undercover. Me, Don and Mike covering the serious business of the Toronto Santa Claus Parade.*

(left) *On polar bear patrol, Churchill, Manitoba. This polar bear is very much alive, just higher than Andrew Scheer at a white party. I left two Aspirins and a glass of water by his head before I left.*

BAD SHOW

I f you're like me, since New Year's, you were waiting desperately for Monday, January 25, to roll around. Last week it finally happened, marking the return of the Forty-Second Parliament. I thought about going up there in person and lining up at midnight so I could actually watch it live, but instead I caught it on TV.

Since then, there have been seven Question Periods. I'm guessing you don't watch every day because, well, you have a life. It's far more likely you've set the PVR so you can binge a whole bunch of them on the weekend. You know, invite over a special friend, Question Period and chill.

I don't want to give away too much, but spoiler alert: This season is awful.

Remember Rona Ambrose? Last season she was minster of health; this season she's leader of the opposition. And remember when she got the job, she said that on her watch the Tories wouldn't heckle and act like spoiled children? Turns out she meant the opposite. They're worse now than they ever were.

And the plot lines this season—totally unbelievable. Like the Conservatives are now mad that the Liberals haven't legalized marijuana yet. That is the most ridiculous plot twist I have ever heard of. Do they think we're stupid? Rona, we remember last season—heck, we remember the past ten seasons. Your party has always said that legalizing pot would mean the end of the world. Now you're upset because you can't get your weed at Costco?

And what's with Tony Clement? Every time he opens his mouth he's saying that governments have to be transparent.

Who are these people fooling? A couple of seasons ago, Tony took fifty million dollars earmarked for border security and secretly spent it on gazebos in Ontario cottage country. I'm sorry, but his character talking about transparency just doesn't ring true.

And then other main characters from last season have been totally written out. According to the credits, Stephen Harper's still in the cast. He has yet to utter a single line. Why are they still paying this guy?

Look, it's early in the season. Granted, I will still keep watching Question Period. And Rona, it's okay to oppose. You are the leader of the opposition. But stop pretending like the past ten years didn't happen. Despite appearances, it's a democratic institution, not a soap opera. You just can't pretend the past decade, *poof*, was all a dream.

NO COMMENT

January 19, 2016

O ver the holidays a buddy of mine—we'll say his name is Bob—was mentioned in a major Canadian magazine. Well, it was their online edition. Why he was mentioned is irrelevant—let's just say it was a slow news day. But because he's a buddy, I read the article. Then I started scrolling through the comments, and sure enough, at the top of page two, someone posted, "Bob is a hypocrite. I hope he dies a painful death." Nice.

It turns out Bob is *not* a hypocrite. He's just a guy who happens to be mentioned in a pretty boring article. Yet for some reason, some guy named Tunnelsnake87 thought it was okay to write and then publish a death threat. And then, for some other reason, it stayed there for days on a website owned by a major Canadian media company. And the reality is, this doesn't surprise us.

If there's an article online, it doesn't matter what the subject is about, it will be followed by comments that are racist, sexist, hate-filled and riddled with spelling mistakes and grammatical errors.

Look, I'm old enough to remember when the internet first happened, and the idea of a comment section after news articles—a virtual debate, as it were—held a lot of promise. No more. The only promise now is that if you read the comments, you will despair for society.

And even though these people are always anonymous, I know exactly who they are. So do you. You can pick them out of a lineup. In fact, you know that famous graphic illustrating the evolution of man? You know the guy on the far right, the one standing up perfectly straight? The dude behind him, slightly bent over—that person. Turns out they have the internet and they're ruining it for all of us.

It is time for serious media organizations to stop the anonymous comments and shut down the online hate. I'm sorry, Tunnelsnake87—put your real name up, or shut up.

NOT JUST JEEPS

January 12, 2016

I love it when political parties get along. In the last federal election, the Tories, the Liberals and the NDP put their differences aside and agreed that none of them, under any circumstances, would question why Canada is now selling arms to Saudi Arabia. It never became an election issue.

And why should it? All we are doing is selling some high-tech armoured military vehicles to our good friend Saudi Arabia. They have a lot of money, they have a huge army and they are number one in the world when it comes to cutting off people's heads. It is literally the easiest place on Earth to get your head cut off. If you're caught doing a magic trick, they will cut off your head. I'm no fan of magic, but what ever happened to old-fashioned booing?

Women are not allowed to drive there. If they're caught driving, they will be convicted and then beaten in public. I would say like a dog, except of course in Canada we don't beat dogs in public.

Why are we in bed like this with Saudi Arabia? Well, Stephen Harper brokered the deal. So his DNA is all over the contract. Of course, that means it's top secret. And the only thing Justin Trudeau has said on the matter is that we are selling them some Jeeps. Really, Justin? Jeeps? Like Barbie used to drive? Did Barbie's jeep have a machine-gun turret? I have to hand it to Justin. Usually prime ministers are on the job for a few years before they start talking down to Canadians. He's learning so fast.

Look, I understand: Selling armoured vehicles to Saudi Arabia means Canadian jobs. And if I were prime minister I don't know if I would have the courage to end a contract this big. But before we embark on any more adventures selling arms to despots, can we agree to debate and discuss it in advance? Because unlike Saudi Arabia, Canada is a free country.

BACK TO SCHOOL

December 1, 2015

In just a matter of days, the Forty-Second Parliament of Canada will begin. For 338 MPs this is not just the first day of school, it's like all the first days wrapped up in one. Think of the pressure. The mood levellers must be flying off the shelves in Ottawa. As they say in pharmaceutical circles, we moved enough antidepressants to feed the entire Conservative caucus.

Stephen Harper is returning to the Hill as a backbench MP. Normally when prime ministers are defeated, they resign. But no, Harper says he is going back and that he'll even show up for work on occasion. Remember that one, kids: If you're ever in a job interview, promise to show up for work on occasion.

One thing we do know about day one, guaranteed: Tom Mulcair will be there, front and centre. Well, not so much front and centre as down the way and off to the side. Tom Mulcair is always fun to watch. Or you could close your eyes and smell the electrical fire in his head.

And then, of course, we have Justin Trudeau. To say that he was a disaster in Question Period while in opposition is an understatement. That boy could not ask a question to save his life. But maybe he'll be good at pretending to answer questions, which is basically what prime ministers do.

But whatever happens in this first week, we must hold our MPs to account. They all promised more civility and less partisanship. Let's not aim for greatness, because that won't happen. But let's set the bar of decorum at an achievable height. Let's aim for grade nine; we'll settle for grade eight. And between you and me, anything above grade six is a win.

A PART OF OUR HERITAGE

November 24, 2015

The Syrian refugee crisis is not the first time Canada has faced something like this. We've done this many times in the past hundred years. Every crisis, of course, is different. But they all have just one thing in common: refugees. Desperate people with nowhere to go. What to do with them?

And there's always a huge debate. It is never black and white; more often than not, it's a sea of grey. Well, imagine for a moment you're walking along the shore next to this sea of grey and you look out and you see someone drowning fifty feet from shore. The question is: Do you throw him the rope? And yes, you have a rope. Of course you'll throw him the rope.

79

But just when you're about to do it, a crowd appears and someone says, "Hey, wait. What do you know about that guy in the water?" And the truth is, you know nothing other than the drowning part. At which point someone says, "How do you even know he's drowning?" Good question. He certainly *looks* like he's drowning. At which point a town car pulls up and out pops a well-dressed man who says, "For the record, I have nothing against throwing the guy a rope, but what's with this arbitrary deadline? What is the rush?" That sets off the heated debates. So heated, in fact, by the time it's over, the guy in the water is underwater. The upside is no rope got wet.

Look, Canada has been here before. In 1979 we accepted sixty thousand Vietnamese boat people. That's us being the good guys. But in 1939 we said no to a ship carrying over nine hundred Jews. We sent them back to Europe. Many perished in concentration camps. That, too, is part of our history. And that's why it's so important we get this one right.

It's 2015. Welcome to Canada.

TO-DO: A TO-DO LIST

November 17, 2015

Many years ago, an executive at WestJet told me that in the early days of that airline, it didn't matter how many flights were delayed or cancelled because the best thing they had going for them, when it came to the public, was that they were not Air Canada. That is what you call a honeymoon period.

That is exactly what is happening to Justin Trudeau right now. He can literally do no wrong. He could wake up tomorrow morning, invoke the War Measures Act, go to lunch, get hammered, back the convertible into a lake and a lot of Canadians would say, "Yeah, okay, but at least he's not as secretive as Stephen Harper was." And I think a lot of people in the media might report the entire incident as a triumph of multitasking.

We are going down a very bad road here. At the risk of coming across as anti-honeymoon, the sooner we all get over this sunny ways business, the better.

Sure, we all like sunny ways and sunny days, but in November the days get pretty short and pretty dark pretty darn fast.

And Justin Trudeau has work to do. A lot of work. According to the *National Post*, the Liberals made 325 promises in the election campaign. That is one heck of a to-do list. And let's face it, honeymoons and to-do lists do not go hand in hand. And we all know the chance of getting anyone to do anything on a to-do list increases dramatically depending on the amount of nagging involved.

So for the country's sake, for the Prime Minister's sake, let's all agree the honeymoon is over. We have moved on to an arranged marriage. Let the nagging begin.

DRIVEN TO DISTRACTION

November 3, 2015

I'm old enough to remember life before Google. I don't know how we survived. The only people who could look anything up at ten o'clock at night were rich people who had the *Encyclopaedia Britannica*. And I'm certainly old enough to remember wandering around with a four-pound cell phone with an antenna so big you could get on a horse and joust with it. But this was long before texting and streaming, and I know it's not fashionable to admit this, but I'm addicted to all of it.

We are slaves to technology. If you're sitting at a red light and you look at the car next to you, you know there's a fifty-fifty chance that person's not looking anywhere at the road. They're staring down at their no-no place and their fingers are going thirty-five miles per hour. In the old days you'd say, "Oh, that's just some clown enjoying a personal moment." But now we know that, no, it's someone who's innocently risking everyone's life while texting in traffic.

We've all done it. *I've* done it. But I don't do it anymore. I have the solution—and it's slightly easier than twelve steps. When I'm behind the wheel, it is the only time in my life that that phone is not near me. It can't be near me. I can't be trusted. If that thing is sitting in the coffee-cup holder and it buzzes, I want to know what's going on. Some part of my lizard brain demands to know what's going on. It could be something really important. Someone could be texting me a picture of their lunch.

So do what I do: Admit you're powerless. Put it in the glove box or put it in the backseat. Depending on your level of addiction, put it in a Ziploc, wrap it in duct tape and lock it in the trunk of the car. Technology is astounding, but please, no more texting in traffic. We all must do what we can to avoid the irony of stupid death by smart phone.

EDITORIAL IDIOCY

October 27, 2015

It's a little too clever to make the statement that print is dead. People have been saying that for a hundred years and yet, every morning, Canadians are reading the newspaper. Five point three million newspapers are sold every single day. But in the final days of the federal election, both national newspapers made it very difficult to wish them any success.

The Globe and Mail surprised nobody by endorsing the Conservatives. Actually, that's not true—an endorsement would have required conviction. Instead, they went the fantasy route. They advised Canadians to vote Conservative to get a Conservative majority and once that happened, Stephen Harper would magically resign. If there were a Pulitzer Prize for the most idiotic editorial ever written, they would win. If there was a second prize for insulting your readership, they would sweep the night.

Then we have the once venerable *National Post*, a paper that has always been rich with opinion. They too endorsed the Conservatives. Which is fine—that is the owner's prerogative. But that's not all they did. On the very same day, they refused to run a column by Andrew Coyne. He had a different opinion. You know Andrew Coyne. He's the guy who is the editor in charge of all of the opinion pieces in the *Post*. He's the reason why we buy the paper in the first place.

Now, if you ask the *Post*, they would say they hired Andrew Coyne because he is the most astute political commentator in the country. Turns out the real reason they hired him was so that, when it mattered the very most, in the final days of the election, they could shut him up. Shame on the *National Post*.

Print is not dead. But with owners like that, it's on life support. Because we all read Coyne anyway. We just did it on Twitter.

NEW HOPE

October 20, 2015

Well, that, my friends, was an election for the ages. The pendulum swung hard. Good men and women were defeated and lots of new folks are heading to Ottawa. But no matter how you voted, no matter whether you were cheering or sobbing a Liberal majority, a new Parliament has been chosen peacefully by the people, and that is worth celebrating.

This will be Canada's forty-second Parliament, and as Canadians we all have to hope it will be the most effective yet.

But of course, that's not up to us. The only people who can make that happen were elected last night.

So I say to all the MPs, regardless of party, remember this: The very best Parliaments were defined not by their size or their shape or the party in power, but by the fact that the individual MPs, when it came down to it, worked together and got along with one another—or at least they tried.

And you know what? Getting along with people is not that hard. It's irritating, but it's doable. And in the real world we all have to get along with people that we don't agree with. It's called finding common ground. It's done in workplaces all across Canada. It's done in families, and it's certainly done in marriages. It's called compromise and respect. And if everyday Canadians can do that, MPs can do that. And if they do, then maybe, just maybe, we will get the best Parliament yet.

So here's to the Forty-Second Parliament of Canada. It's a blank slate. She has yet to disappoint.

THE END OF BIG THINKING
October 13, 2015

For weeks now, the Canadian Press has been doing a wonderful thing. It is compiling all of the promises of the main contenders for the job of prime minister, and it is a great resource. Because when you see all the promises in one place and you get the big picture, wow! . . . It is completely underwhelming. If you strung all the promises together in the form of a Final Jeopardy! question, the answer would be, "What is a lack of vision?"

Don't get me wrong. Some of the promises are inspiring. I am pleased to see that the Prime Minister promised to start protecting wild turkey habitat in 2017. Very happy. It made me want to get a lawn sign. But looking at that promise and so many similar ones, I can't help but think: If Stephen Harper had been prime minister back in the day, would he have championed something big like the creation of medicare? Is he the kind of guy who would say, "Let's build a national railway?" Because he has been prime minister for ten years, and I can't picture him building the bridge to PEI.

It's like the notion of nation building is gone. We are in the middle of an election campaign, and there's no talk of making Canada better or fairer. Instead we have a prime minister promising to stop anyone from wearing a niqab in the civil service, even though nobody has ever asked to do so—ever, since Confederation. We are literally supposed to get together and get angry about a woman in a niqab who works at the Department of Fisheries who doesn't even exist.

Governing Canada has always meant creating a big tent. Suddenly we're a small tent with a dress code. They call this "boutique politics." Perfect word. Boutiques are small and for certain people only. Nation building is for everyone and means thinking big.

BAD NEWS FOR DEMOCRACY

March 31, 2015

I love Samara Canada. It's an amazing charity. Its entire reason for being is to inspire Canadians to become more involved in democracy. What's not to love? They aren't stuffy, they've got a great sense of humour. If you love politics, you could spend hours on their website.

But if you love democracy, it can be kind of depressing. Samara's latest report card is out, and its message is clear: If Canadian democracy were a patient, it would be in the hallway on a gurney on its way to palliative care.

Turns out the majority of Canadians are completely disgusted by our politics. If this keeps up, the only people who will ever vote are the base. The base, by the way, no matter which party you're talking about, are a group of blindly loyal drones who live to get a Christmas card from their MP. As I said, fairly depressing.

But there is good news. Canadians are incredibly active and generous. A healthy majority gives money to charity or devotes time to causes they believe in. They want to be engaged. They just don't want to be engaged to anyone on Parliament Hill.

I just spent an entire week surrounded by young people age six to twenty-six who want nothing more than to make the world a better place. But if you suggest they join a political party, you might as well tell them to go slam their head in a locker. When it comes to politics, abstinence is on the rise.

So, to the leaders of the major political parties, this is go time. Canadians, especially young Canadians—they're just not that into you. There's less than one year until the next federal election. Please, look beyond your bases. Because democracy is far too important to sacrifice to partisan politics.

THE MONUMENT MEN

March 17, 2015

Ottawa has twenty-four national monuments and memorials, all different shapes and sizes. The largest and most prominent monument in the nation's capital is the National War Memorial. Now Ottawa is getting another monument. It's yet to be built. It will honour the victims of communism. Entirely appropriate, but everything about this story is completely bizarre.

For starters, it came out of nowhere. This was the brainchild of two cabinet ministers, Jason Kenney and then John Baird. These boys have big egos, so this won't be just any monument. This is going to be huge. If they were going to have their names on it, it had to be bigger and more imposing than the National War Memorial. I'm sorry, that's just weird.

The thing covers an entire city block downtown. The land alone is worth thirty million dollars. The land was supposed to be for a federal court building. Kenney and Baird went in behind closed doors and the site was theirs. Now, is this on the up and up? I don't know. But they kept the land transfer secret for an entire year—what does that tell you? The whole thing is shrouded in so much mystery, it's like they've taken inspiration from the communist countries the memorial is condemning.

John Baird says the people of Ottawa want this. Personally, I think the people of Ottawa want a hockey rink that's not thirty-six kilometres away. But that's another story.

What is true is that this government, for all its talk of transparency, allowed two cabinet ministers to decide, without any consultation, that the War Memorial should be a poor cousin. This is nothing but a nervous government trying desperately to cement itself in history before it's too late. This is not how grown-up countries act.

GIVE IT AWAY

March 10, 2015

Do you know what I am eternally grateful for and yet don't like to think about very much? My organs. Out of sight, out of mind has always been my philosophy. Don't get me wrong: I'm glad my organs are in there, doing whatever it is they're supposed to do. I'm just not particularly attached to them.

When the day comes that I don't need them, I hope someone else can use them. This does not make me unique. Eighty-nine percent of Canadians support the idea of organ donation. We are a generous, intelligent people. We are also a nation of procrastinators. We view organ donation the same way we view cleaning up the basement: We support the idea, but it's just very easy to put it off until, well, forever.

And every province is different. I assumed that I was a donor because I live in Ontario and I checked "Take 'em all" on my driver's licence years ago. Turns out that's no guarantee—I'm also supposed to register online. And no matter where you live, if your second cousin twice removed shows up at the last minute saying no, then your kidneys aren't going anywhere. And if you live in one province and you get hit by a truck in another, who knows what's going to happen.

There is a solution: a national registry. We should have an app for that. Sadly, we live in a country where no government, federal or provincial, has any interest in doing anything that everyone can get behind, because there's no political points in that. That's not going to change soon. Let's face it: If any of our organs goes on the fritz tomorrow, we're all going to want to be on the list to get a new one. Well, it works both ways.

Take a few minutes, talk it out with your family. Figure out how it works in your province and make sure that when you leave, you don't take your organs with you.

THE FRIGHTENERS

March 3, 2015

Which great political leader was it who said, "The only thing we have to fear is fear itself"? Well, you can Google that later, but we know for certain it wasn't Stephen Harper. He loves to remind us over and over again that danger is lapping at our shores.

These days there are a lot of things to be afraid of. The government and the media are constantly telling us that terrorism is at the top of that list, and so it should be. But that is just the tip of the iceberg.

Danger is not just lapping at our shores, it's in the

bathroom. Do you have any idea how many bad things can happen to you in the bathroom? People die in there every year—hundreds of them. And I for one would welcome it if, from now on, in every speech the Prime Minister gave, he would go on at length about the dangers of slip and fall. Any discussion about the economy should be met with tough talk on how to keep us safe in the bathroom.

And we need new powers, new laws forcing Canadians to use those rubber bath mats. And there is no time to debate these laws, and obviously the state will need new powers to enter the bathroom. If Peter MacKay or Jason Kenney wants in your toilet—upstairs or down—that is a small price to pay.

And while we're on the subject, do you have any idea how many Canadians are killed every year in the summer? It is our deadliest season. And yet we are encouraged to go outdoors. That needs a rethink.

If you go online and you research all the frightening things in this world, you would realize that Stephen Harper is right. We have every reason to be afraid. But if we give in to that fear, we would never debate a bill, go outdoors or take a shower again.

Before bed, Prime Minister Harper read to me from the Accountability Act, his signature piece of legislation. Fairy tales or fantasy fiction can always put me to sleep.

Don, Mike, me and John at the summit in Gros Morne National Park, Newfoundland and Labrador. I am wearing Parks Canada gear because it is slimming.

My job description included jumping into frigid water on a regular basis. Here I am spending New Year's Day on the wharf in Herring Cove, Nova Scotia, with comedian Ron James. Hello, North Atlantic.

TURNING AGAINST TOURISM

February 10, 2015

These are confusing times for the Canadian economy. When the dollar is low, there are winners and there are losers. One thing we all understand is that a low dollar is good for the tourism industry. But you can't have a tourism industry without advertising. Look at those Newfoundland tourism ads—boy, have they ever paid off. Tourism is now a billion-dollar industry in Newfoundland. Yes, with a *B*.

So now with our low dollar, you can only imagine how much money the federal government is spending in the United States, promoting Canada as a tourism destination. And we all know how much this government loves to advertise. Take a guess: How much are they spending? Wait for it: zero dollars. The United States is Canada's largest tourism market, and two years ago the Harper government decided to stop advertising there.

I don't know what's more astounding: that the feds are getting out of tourism or that Elizabeth May is the only politician actually talking about this. And I admit, when I first heard Ms. May say this, I didn't believe her because, you know, Green Party. But I checked. She's telling the truth.

Apparently, in 2015, telling people to visit Canada is very old-fashioned and unbecoming of an energy superpower. In the year 2000 Canada was among the ten most visited countries in the world. Now we are eighteenth.

Tourism is not ideological. There's no left-wing and right-wing view of tourism. There *is* a defeatist view, and our government has one.

WAR ON VETERANS

Three years ago the Harper government went to court in a fight with Canadian veterans. The government argued that if a disabled veteran was compensated for, say, losing a limb, then the government should be able to claw back that money out of their pension. Thankfully, the courts ruled that no, the government can't take pension money away from the disabled, because losing a limb is not the same as getting a bonus at work.

Now we find out that once again the government's in court, fighting veterans, and this time they've spent seven hundred thousand dollars. And their argument is simple: that Canada has no obligation to veterans whatsoever. None whatsoever. They admit that, yes, prior to the Battle of Vimy Ridge, Prime Minister Sir Robert Borden promised that Canada had a sacred obligation to veterans. But our government is saying that's no longer true. No obligation at all. Now, sadly, for anyone who knows veterans, or disabled ones, this comes as no surprise.

My buddy Paul is a veteran. He lost both his legs in Afghanistan. Every year they make him prove over and over again that his legs are still gone. Four times they've said, "Nope, we're not taking your word for it. You have to prove they're still gone. Get a note from a doctor." Literally a note saying his legs have not grown back. You know, in case he's pulling a fast one. His friend was shot in the head and has to prove over and over again that he still has no vision in his left eye. His left eye, by the way, is made out of glass.

So the next time you bump into an MP and they're telling you how much this government does for veterans, don't take them at their word. Tell them to prove it.

ECONOMIC BEWILDERMENT

January 27, 2015

There's nothing I hate more than those situations where, the more I read, the more confused I become. Welcome to the Canadian economy. Five minutes ago the government was crystal clear: It was all about the oil. It was practically government policy that every first-born child in Canada should become a pipefitter. If anyone dared suggest that our economy was too dependent on oil, they were nothing less than an enemy of the state.

And now the price of oil has tanked, the world is dumping our currency and Prime Minister Harper is showing up in Ontario, of all places, talking about manufacturing. Yes, Alberta, I hate to break it to you, but Big Daddy's flitting around eastern Canada saying, "Oil-shmoil, I barely knew her." Give him another week, he'll be admitting he was born and raised in Toronto.

This is why I am so confused. The Bank of Canada says low oil prices are very bad for Canada. All of Canada. And yet the government is saying there are tax breaks for the wealthy coming and everything is on budget. But oh . . . wait . . . there is no budget. How can there be no budget? You know why there's no budget? Because behind the dull eyes of the finance minister is a brain melting in full-blown panic.

Look, I lived in Newfoundland before the collapse of the fishery; I understand how upset people in Alberta are. But one thing we know is no matter what happens, we will get through this together. As sure as the sun will rise, the sun will set, and there will be very expensive commercials on TV, paid for by us, telling us—wait for it—that our economy is the envy of the world.

TALK AMONGST YOURSELVES

On January 30, every premier and territorial leader in Canada will gather in Ottawa for a meeting. Imagine, all those leaders in one room, behind closed doors. They call it the Council of the Federation. And once again the Prime Minister of Canada will not attend that meeting. He's been invited, but he said no. He will not pose for a photo; he will not engage in small talk about hockey, the weather or plunging oil prices. And nor should he. He's got six episodes of *Murdoch Mysteries* in his PVR that he needs to catch up on.

Of course, the premiers don't like the fact that the Prime Minister refuses to meet with them again. He hasn't met with them in six years. But if you read any great book by any great leader, they will tell you that the last thing you should ever do is get all the decision makers together in one room. That could lead to discussion, and even solutions.

And as a leader, the other thing you must never do is engage in frank talk with people who have been elected to represent every part of the nation. It's that kind of thinking that led to the creation of Canada in the first place.

And what I cannot abide is the suggestion that the Prime Minister is afraid to meet the premiers. That is a low blow. He's not afraid to meet the premiers; he just has no interest in anything they have to say on any subject.

So let the premiers go off and busy themselves with the silly work of nation building. My Canada includes my Prime Minister, across the street, at home, alone, in the dark.

NO WORDS

January 13, 2015

On the morning of October 22, Corporal Nathan Cirillo was gunned down while guarding the Tomb of the Unknown Soldier at the National War Memorial. In the weeks after the shooting, there were probably ten million words written about that incident. Yet nothing came closer to capturing the mood of the nation than the cartoon published the very next morning in the Halifax *Chronicle Herald*. The artist is Bruce MacKinnon. He is one of Canada's greatest editorial cartoonists, and we have a lot of them in this country. Which is why, every week, in every newspaper in Canada, there are letters from people who are deeply offended by a cartoon. That is what comes with opinion.

In all my years of wandering around, spouting off in an alley, I have gotten hundreds of emails from people who were offended for one reason or another. And yet I can't remember one that said I didn't have a right to my opinion. They said I was stupid, wrong, pigheaded, ignorant, yes, but no death threats. The most I've had to deal with was a late-night drunk dial from an agitated cabinet minister.

How lucky are we that we live in a country where, when offended, that's what we do—send an email or leave a rambling voice message. Like most people who move around upright, I have beliefs. I'd like to think I have beliefs that I would die for. The freedom to offend is very near the top. Thankfully, for me personally that has never been put to the test. It was put to the test this past week in Paris when the offices of a magazine known for its outrageous editorial cartoons were attacked by two men with machine guns. There were 11 fatalities.

Honestly, I can't put into words how I feel about what happened. But when I go online and I see the editorial cartoons created in the aftermath, I don't have to.

THE RIGHT (AND LEFT) THING TO DO

December 2, 2014

I have a question that's been bothering me for a while now. Well, actually, it's been bothering me since about eight o'clock this morning, when I was almost crushed by an SUV on my way to work.

When did using a turn signal become optional in this country?

Remember the turn signal? That little stick on the left-hand side of the steering wheel? I say "remember" because I'm guessing a lot of Canadians have no idea what that stick is or what it's used for.

If aliens came down from outer space and studied the way Canadians drive, they would assume that using a turn signal was a voluntary exercise and that there were no firm guidelines surrounding its use.

Refresher: It's to signal people. It tells others what you're about to do before you do it. Which comes in handy at 110 kilometres an hour. And all of you people who use it to tell people what you've done after you've done it? You are doing it wrong.

And to you, the guy in the intersection who decides at the last minute to turn left but believes there is no reason in the world to tell anyone what you're up to or why you've suddenly stopped on a green light: You, sir, are not only a bad driver, you're a bad person. How bad? Everyone around you hates you. But don't worry, I can help you. There's a simple solution.

Signal.

It's as easy as lifting a finger. Literally. So this holiday season, save a life, lift a finger. So the rest of us don't have to show you ours.

PARTISAN INFERNO

November 25, 2014

Dante's *Inferno*, a very famous fourteenth-century epic poem, describes Dante's descent into hell. According to Dante, there are nine circles of suffering. And as one can imagine, they get worse as you go on and on. Spoiler alert: The final circle is basically sitting in a room, watching Canada Action Plan ads over and over again on a loop.

By now, everyone is familiar with these ads. You can't watch a hockey game or an episode of *Steven and Chris* in this country without a Canada Action Plan ad telling you to love your government because your government loves you. My favourite is the one that tells us how much our government loves and cares for our veterans. I swear to you, if I have a stroke in the next twelve months, it will be while I'm watching one of those commercials.

Governments are not supposed to spend taxpayers' money on ads promoting their own party or their election platform. End of story.

I'm not saying this government is the first one to do it—far from it. But let's give credit where credit is due: They have turned it into a fine art. They have spent over 620 million tax dollars on such advertising since they've been elected. Partisan advertising has become like doping in sports: Those who do it, defend it. But we all know it's designed to give one party an unfair edge. And we all know it's cheating.

Canada's Action Plan. The only thing honest is the title. Canada—I know what that means. And I know what "action" the government's doing to us when they put those ads on TV. I would draw a picture, but that, you can't show in prime time.

GROUND CONTROL TO THE GOVERNMENT OF CANADA

November 18, 2014

Last week I was looking at my Facebook feed when my friend updated his status to read, "One hour ago, humanity successfully landed a spacecraft on a slowly tumbling mountain of ice and rock—let's celebrate." It was a nice break from your classic updates, such as "I'm eating pizza!" or "My cat is possessed." Since then, like so many people, I've become obsessed with what a group of European science geeks have been up to in outer space.

The numbers alone make my brain hurt. They landed a spacecraft on a comet that is half a billion kilometres away. It took ten years to get there, and the comet is moving at 135,000 kilometres an hour.

For thousands of years, people trembled in fear when a comet appeared in our sky. And now, in 2014, we have visited one. What an astounding thing humanity has accomplished, all in the name of pure science. And my God, how smart must the men and women be who pulled this thing off?

And how sad that here on Earth, or at least on our little part of it in Canada, pure science is no longer encouraged. We have a government that not only abolished the Office of the National Science Advisor, but bragged about it. In Canada, the only time you hear about scientists now is when they're being told to shut up or they're being shut down by a government that can't even begin to understand what the scientists are talking about.

I don't know much about science, but I know this: They didn't land a spaceship on a comet using anecdotal evidence, and they didn't calibrate the rate of descent using focus groups. Canadians get excited about pure science. Canadians are as passionate and as curious as anyone else. It's our government that begs to differ.

TWELVE MONTHS OF THIS

November 4, 2014

The Prime Minister was in Vaughan, Ontario, this past week. The tie was gone; he was in his groovy relaxed mode, which personally I find to be his most unsettling personality. But he was there to make promises about income splitting.

Afterwards, he invited the media to stick around and have some sandwiches and watch him do arts and crafts with children. Because you know Stephen Harper—nothing makes him happier than getting out the Crayolas and getting down on the ground with the little ones. When they spit up—that's his happy place.

This is hot on the heels of Tom Mulcair and the NDP inviting the media along to see Tom up on the monkey bars with toddlers while he made promises. Because you know Tom Mulcair: Everything about that man screams, "Let's all get in the bouncy castle!" Next week Justin Trudeau will appear at a daycare, also making promises and simultaneously juggling three infants and a puppy.

This is it, Canada. As predicted in the prophecies, when the pale ones appear on the playgrounds, the election campaign has begun. And we are twelve months out. Canada has always been blessed with short election campaigns— historically, five or six weeks, max, which is a good thing.

The one thing that every election campaign since Confederation has in common is this: Nothing of any substance gets accomplished during a campaign. Of course not. The leaders are too busy to lead. Sorry, no time to govern; I have to go get photographed feigning interest in a cow.

We are now looking down the barrel at twelve months of these three men, promising us the sun, the moon and the stars while wearing hard hats, cowboy hats, hair nets and stilettos. It's like a never-ending episode of *So You Think You Can Govern Canada*, except we can't change the channel because the country is on remote control.

OPEN HOUSE

October 28, 2014

When Canadians visit Ottawa—and all Canadians should at some point in their lives—without fail they'll make it up to Parliament Hill. Which makes perfect sense; the buildings are spectacularly beautiful. They are my favourite buildings in the entire country.

I promise you, if you make it up there an hour before sunset, when the golden light is dancing on the Peace Tower, it is an experience you will never forget. Even in the pouring rain, in the sleet or the snow, in the middle of winter, thirty below, the sight can still make your heart skip. Parliament Hill, as they say in the world of real estate, shows beautifully.

And when I'm talking to people about visiting Ottawa, I always say the same thing: Take the tour. Because Canadians, being Canadians, sometimes don't think about lining up and going inside. But there are tours almost every day. The hours vary, but they're open pretty much all year round. And it's been like that for over a hundred years.

And when you get inside, the walls are dripping in history. And the tour guides, all full-time students, are so young, informed and well-spoken, you can't help but think that this generation is the best and the brightest yet.

And unlike similar tours of similar buildings elsewhere in the world, the access is spectacular. The first time I took a tour, I remember thinking, "Wow, we are walking around like we own the joint." And of course, we do.

It's our house. It's on a hill. And there's a tower. And it's named for the idea, the concept and notion of peace. And it's open to all of us. Times change, but that never has. Let's keep our heads and ensure that it never will.

BE THERE FOR NURSES

October 21, 2014

Recently I attended a graduation at York University. You cannot help but be moved, watching a parade of young people who have worked so hard as they march across the stage and pick up their bachelor of this or their master's of that—young graduates filled with such hope, such promise—and such crushing personal debt.

The last group to graduate were the nurses. They are a tribe unto themselves. They were by far the loudest of the bunch. They didn't care; they cheered each other on louder and harder than anyone else. They celebrated as if nobody was watching. They had the best shoes. And as they strode across that stage, I could not help but think what kind of occupation are they marching into.

We've all seen the news. We live on a continent that is currently hysterical about a terrible disease that very few of us know anything about. And we've been here before. In my lifetime, AIDS happened; good people, decent people, family and friends were scared and ran the other way. Nurses—they went into the room, they held the hands. When SARS happened, when the city of Toronto was bathing in Purell, the nurses went to work every day. And when they got sick, other nurses replaced them.

And now we have this terrible thing, Ebola. It has yet to (and perhaps never will) reach our shores. But if it does, we know what will happen. We will run for the hills, they will run into the room.

So let us take a moment and praise the nurses. And let it be known that in this country, in Canada, no nurse should be denied the equipment or training they need to do their job safely. We should be there for the nurses, because they're always there for us.

STEALING IS WRONG FOR TORIES TOO

October 14, 2014

When a three- or four-year-old picks up candy in the corner store and puts it in their pocket without paying for it, we all understand it's not the end of the world. And we also understand that if that child has parents with a moral compass, then on that day that child learns the lesson that stealing is wrong. Because in our society, if you take something that does not belong to you without permission, it is theft. It does not matter who you are.

Unless, of course, you're the Conservative Party of Canada, which recently floated the idea of changing Canada's copyright laws. Not to protect people who need the laws or to create jobs. No, no. They want to change the laws to allow political parties—them, specifically—to take news footage that they don't own, to re-edit it, slow it down, add creepy music and create attack ads. Well, in this country, you just can't do that to footage without permission, no matter how tempting the candy is—because it is stealing. If Global TV, a private news outfit, invests time, energy, resources and money landing an exclusive interview, another news network can't take that footage and put it on TV. Because they don't own it. A charity can't put that on TV because they don't own it. There are no exceptions. To quote a very popular document: Thou shalt not steal. I know Stephen Harper has been accused of having a hidden agenda, but I didn't think it involved circumventing the Ten Commandments.

Stealing is wrong. If the Tories allow this to go through, every Tory MP should have to write a letter to the children in their ridings explaining to them why, the next time they're in a store, if they think they can get away with it and no one is looking, they can take all the candy they want.

BOUND BY TRADITION?

October 7, 2014

When I was growing up my father always told me that when they went to work every day, the vast majority of Canadians tried their best. That it was human nature to do so. And you know what? I believed him. Well, with all due respect, I can't help but think that when my father came to that conclusion, it was before there were cameras in the House of Commons.

We have gotten to the point now where if you ask this government any question on any issue, domestic or international, they will tell you, "We stand with Israel." You ask a cabinet minister directions to the closest washroom, and they will tell you, "We stand with Israel." Which, personally, I believe does a disservice to Israel. But that is the situation we find ourselves in.

Enter the Speaker of the House of Commons, our referee, our saviour of democracy, Andrew Scheer. He says it is not his job to ensure that the government answers direct questions in Question Period—despite the fact that it's been in his job description since 1894.

Well, that's not the way Scheer sees it. No, in a passionate, passionate ruling, he revealed to the country that his only role is to ensure decorum in the House of Commons. Show me one person who believes he's done a good job on the decorum front. Three hundred and eight meth addicts on the dance floor have better manners.

Which brings me to a proposal. This government is always saying it's looking for redundancies to save money in government. May I suggest the job of Speaker, a job that comes with a minister's salary, a staff, a car, a driver, a house in the country where deer gambol on the lawn—yes, they gambol—and we replace the Speaker with a bag of flour with a smiley face drawn on the front with a Sharpie. What's the worst thing that could happen? Questions will go unanswered? Rudeness will prevail?

Because, really, if the highlight of one's professional career is an eloquent explanation as to why they are useless, they should be relieved of the burden of faking it.

THE KIDS ARE ONLINE

April 1, 2014

One of the advantages of a majority government is that it can pretty much do whatever it wants. How we ended up with a strong, stable majority government with just 39 percent of the popular vote is just a fun fact of Canadian democracy.

But with voter turnouts at historic lows, everyone realizes that our democratic process needs some tinkering. Which is why the government has introduced the Fair Elections Act. Ironic title, because in a clever move this government has decided the way to deal with low voter turnout is to make voting more difficult. Got to hand it to them. Did not see that coming.

How is it possible in 2014, in a bill that deals with how we can vote, there was absolutely no discussion of online voting?

And I know, online voting makes a lot of Canadians very nervous. I'm one of them. I'm old-fashioned. I like the notion of lining up in a church basement, getting a little stubby pencil and marking an X. And do you know what that makes me? A dinosaur.

Because while I may not like the idea of online voting, I know who will love the idea: young Canadians. They are some of the most wired people on the planet. They go to school online, they work online—heck, they find husbands and wives online. There are literally millions of young Canadians who have never walked across the room to an attractive person and tried to score a phone number, because there's an app for that. If the biological imperative won't get them out of the house, I don't know how voting is going to do it.

The government has a responsibility to make voting available wherever Canadians live. And yes, all Canadians reside in a riding, but young Canadians live online. If we let them pay taxes there, let them vote there.

SPLIT DECISION
March 25, 2014

Hats off to Jim Flaherty. Canada's finance minister has left the building after eight years on the job, and I for one am going to miss the guy. Because no matter what you think of Jim Flaherty, I can say this: He was never afraid to speak his own mind. Which is why, on the way out the door, he made it pretty clear that the government's plan for income splitting is a bad idea.

This was a bombshell in Tory circles because income splitting is the biggest promise that Stephen Harper made in the last election. And on paper it looks great. I mean, the government is going to take three billion dollars that hard-working Canadians paid in taxes and just give it back. What's not to like? Well, the problem is in the fine print. Jim Flaherty, he saw the fine print. Turns out the vast majority of Canadians, 85 percent, will not see a dime. Although we're all going to have to pay for the TV commercials telling us how great it is.

Income splitting is a massive tax break, no doubt about it. The problem is, the people who will benefit the most are married couples with young children where one parent makes a lot of money and the other parent stays home. Someone like . . . I don't know . . . who would be the poster child, the poster boy for this tax break? It would be Stephen Harper! There you go. He's an average Canadian. He has a big job, makes a lot of money, his wife volunteers, he has lovely children. God bless him, he deserves a raise, and with this tax break, he's gonna give himself one.

Now, who's *not* going to see any money? That would be everyone else. Those couples where both work like dogs but neither are rich. Single dads? Single moms? Sorry, no breaks for you.

Stephen Harper has said that this is an excellent tax break designed to help Canadian families. Well, I can't believe this needs to be said in 2014, Prime Minister, but families come in all different shapes and sizes. And here's an idea: If you're going to give a tax cut, how about giving one to all Canadians, and not just Canadians who look like you?

AMICABLE FANTASY

March 18, 2014

I guess, as happens in so many marriages, we all just got a bit complacent. It has been twenty years since the last Quebec referendum. We can't be blamed for thinking that those marriage troubles were behind us. I mean, yes, we had that rough patch there in 1995, when Quebec wanted to see other people, but we got through that. And now, all of a sudden, we turn on the news every night and there's Pauline Marois talking about an independent Quebec.

I'm not saying the marriage is over; we've got a long way to go before we get there. But you just know there's going to be a whole lot of awfully touchy-feely conversations in our future. That and the throwing of dishes. Because, just like the last time we were in marriage counselling, the Parti Québécois is completely delusional. I mean, to hear Pauline Marois tell it, this divorce would not just be amicable, it would be downright pleasant. I mean, Quebec is going to be this wonderful country without borders and no tolls, and they're going to use the Canadian dollar—and oh, they're going to have a seat on the board of directors of the Bank of Canada. Really, Pauline? Anything else we can get ya?

The Parti Québécois is like some guy in a bar telling his friends he's going to leave his wife, except he's going to keep the house and the dog *and* they're going to sleep with each other when he's in the mood. And oh, she's going to take over the car payments. See, in the real world, that guy would have friends there to give him a smack and tell him he was an idiot. But in the fantasy world of Quebec politics, these notions go completely unchallenged.

Look, we all know there are troubles in most marriages. And some marriages, sadly, end in divorce. And an amicable divorce is the best kind of divorce. And if you believe they exist—I've got a bridge to sell you. It's well constructed and located in Quebec.

EVERYTHING BUTT THE TRUTH

March 11, 2014

The very worst thing that anyone can do in the House of Commons, believe it or not, is to suggest, or even hint, that an MP is lying. If you do that and you do not apologize immediately, the Speaker will throw you out of the House. And the reason why it's such a no-no is because members of Parliament are such upstanding members of society that they would never intentionally lie to the House. Meanwhile, back on planet Earth, we know better.

Last month, Tory MP Brad Butt stood in the House and

said that he had witnessed widespread voter fraud in his riding. He saw it—he saw rival campaign workers pluck voter ID cards out of the blue bins and then use them to commit voter fraud. He used the phrases "I saw" and "I witnessed" five separate times. Shocking allegations. Except . . . a complete lie. He just made it up to make his government's legislation look better. He just made it up.

Bear in mind, MPs take an oath of allegiance before they take their seat in the House of Commons. And it's serious. It's like being on the stand, swearing on your mother's grave and a double pinky swear all wrapped up in one. In the real world, if you're caught lying, there are consequences. If you do it in court, you go to jail. If you do it on the job, you get fired. A seven-year-old understands this. They may not get fired, but they would get a time out. But not Brad, oh no. All Brad had to do was stand up and, like a sulking adolescent, say, "I did not mean to mislead the House." Ironically, he said this in the House—another lie in the House.

I have to believe in my heart of hearts that MPs, most of them, would not intentionally lie. But it is getting harder and harder to be shocked when they do. Because without any consequences, the House is becoming more and more common and less and less honourable every day.

JUSTIN, JUST DON'T

March 4, 2014

When Justin Trudeau became leader of the Liberal party, there were a lot of unknowns. People wondered, and rightly so, "Does he have the right stuff to lead?" And now he's riding high in the polls and he's made one thing crystal clear: Justin Trudeau is a master of the art of the apology. No surprise, really. As they say, practice makes perfect.

Last week he apologized for making a lame joke about hockey during a discussion about the crisis in Ukraine; before that, he apologized to Alberta; before that, the used car salesmen of Canada; before that, Peter Kent, because when Peter Kent was Harper's environment minister, Justin called him a piece of . . . well, you get the idea. And clearly, three out of these four apologies were warranted.

What I find fascinating is that Trudeau doesn't get in trouble because of his ideas; he gets in trouble when he tries to be funny. Now, maybe he is funny one on one—I have no idea—but I know this: When Ukraine comes up in the conversation, that's not the time to reach for the seltzer bottle.

This is a problem that affects all political parties. Leaders surround themselves with people who will not tell them the truth. Is there no one in that super brain trust the Liberal party apparently has who can say, "Hey Justin, remember that you're applying for the job of prime minister of Canada, not open-mic night at the Giggle Barn"? Hey, there's worse things in life, Justin. Accept it: You're tall and handsome and not that amusing. We should all be so lucky.

And all parties are guilty of this. Is there not a single adviser
in the Prime Minister's Office honest enough to say, "Hey

Prime Minister, great job in the House of Commons today, and uh, one more thing, you're a horrible singer, so stop doing that."

We all need to take a breath and remember that these are mortal leaders, not kings. And if a bad joke or a butchered Beatles song can't be stopped? Who's going to kill the truly bad ideas?

MINISTER OF STATE FOR DEMOCRATIC REDUCTION

February 25, 2014

D o you ever have those days where you feel like there's a higher power whose entire purpose is to constantly test your grip on reality? You know, the kind of day when you wake up and hear that Pierre Poilievre has been chosen by Prime Minister Harper to reform democracy in Canada. I mean, on a day like that, it's entirely normal to think, "I must be hallucinating." Because I guarantee you, if you get any member of the Conservative caucus alone in a room and ask them, "Who is the last man on Earth who should be put in charge of reforming democracy?" they will tell you: Pierre Poilievre.

But the Prime Minister gave him a job to do and boy, has he done it. He has tabled the Fair Elections Act. And I promise you, if you read this bill you will feel like you have left Canada and slipped into a parallel universe. When this bill passes it will be illegal for Elections Canada to encourage young people to vote. Because, well, there's the problem right there, isn't it? I mean, you get young people voting, and the next thing you know you have an entire generation of informed citizens running around, taking part in democracy and feeling a real sense of ownership in Canada.

If you ask the government, it will tell you voter turnout in Canada is at a historic low, and that's proof that encouraging people to vote does not work. Not true. People do not vote because they look at the way that politics is being performed in Canada and they feel like they've been given a feed of bad oysters. After that, they just avoid the buffet altogether.

We Canadians love to brag that we are one of the world's greatest democracies. If we abandon the principle that voting is important and must be encouraged, we forfeit the title.

DISRESPECTING OUR VETERANS

February 4, 2014

It's been an open secret for years now that our country has been involved in a covert war against veterans. Now, don't get me wrong; in some ways the government loves veterans—they look great in a photo op. What it doesn't like are veterans as a budget line. Because veterans, especially disabled ones, cost a lot of money. So now, with new vets— say, from Afghanistan—who are injured or disabled, our government likes to give them a one-time lump-sum payment, no fuss, no muss, and then you're on your own. And don't call us, my friend, when the money runs out. Remember, our Prime Minister likes to fancy himself a bit of an economist.

Then we have our Second World War vets; fewer of them are using Veterans Affairs offices. We lose over one thousand World War II vets every single month in this country. That's what economists call a downward trend. And really, how many of them are going to be around for the next election? So let's just shut their offices right now.

If there's a hero in this covert battle, it would have to be Veterans Affairs Minister Julian Fantino for dragging this entire conflict out in the open. Recently veterans from all over Canada travelled to Ottawa to meet with the minister to discuss these issues in a scheduled meeting. Well, the eighty-eight-year old who fought the Nazis managed to make it on time. The soldier from Afghanistan with the shrapnel in his brain managed to make it on time. Whereas Fantino was a no-show. He let those soldiers wait down the hallway for over an hour. Then he waltzes by, gets mad at them and then walks out in a huff. Julian, you're a public servant. Try acting like one.

In some battles, you have to choose sides, and when it comes to government versus veterans, it's hard to go with the government when they're not even offering common courtesy or respect.

WINTER REALLY IS COMING

I have come to the conclusion that when it comes to winter, Canadians—at least those of us that live in the cities—suffer from a seasonal amnesia. When it snows or gets cold, or when the rain turns to ice and it gets slippery, it comes as a complete and total shock. We like to think we're good at winter, but we're not anymore. And it seems like every year we're all getting worse.

I took an informal poll, and it turns out that I know people who live in this country, in this city, where today it is twenty-seven below, who don't own a single pair of long underwear. Whereas my grandfather's generation wore long underwear every day for six months straight, so he probably had two pairs.

And I'm just as bad. I was away from Toronto over the holidays when the power went out. And after three days I was worried my pipes might freeze. And my father looked at me with total confusion and said, "It's the winter. Why didn't you drain your pipes before you left?" And I'm like, "I didn't drain my pipes before I left because I don't live in the Dark Ages." Not a very good comeback when the city you live in has no power. And it's not like I don't know any better. I have lived through half a dozen ice storms. I know what to expect, and yet I was completely unprepared. It's not climate change I'm worried about, it's memory change.

So the next time I leave, I will be prepared. The pipes will be drained, the long johns will be packed and I don't want to cause panic, but one of these days I might get myself a box of emergency candles. So let's say it together, people: This is not new. It's not a polar vortex. It happens every year. It's called winter.

MONEY FOR NOTHING

January 21, 2014

My new year's resolution this year was to be more Zen. I look at my father. Stuff doesn't bother him, and I admire that. Specifically, I resolved not to get so angry at my government—to always give them the benefit of the doubt and to look at both sides. Total failure. I might as well have resolved to grow a third arm.

My problem was, and I see this now, that if I wanted to remain Zen, I should have resolved to avoid the news altogether. Because in this country that's all it takes. Five minutes of any newscast is enough to send any rational Canadian into such an intense rage spiral, you've got to hold on to your ears to stop your head from popping off.

This past week the numbers were released. Our government spent $2.5 million advertising a job creation program that does not exist. As in, it is fiction. It's a pretend thing. Two point five million dollars advertising something that is not real. Just saying it out loud sounds like the ravings of a mad person.

In the private sector if a company did that, it would be called false advertising. It's a criminal offence. If Ford Motors advertised a car that runs on water and floats on air in the middle of the Super Bowl, the president would be fired—and then institutionalized.

Meanwhile, the very real cabinet minister in charge of pretend programs, Jason Kenney, says it is money well spent. And the Prime Minister agrees. Apparently, they had a secret meeting in a fort they made out of couch cushions, they read *The Emperor's New Clothes* by flashlight, and missed the point of the fairy tale and thought it made for good economic policy. Why not? Entirely plausible.

We have entered a world of unicorns and magic beans. The only reason a government would advertise a program that does not exist is because they believed people were too stupid to tell the difference or were too beaten to care. And if we don't get angry about this one, they will be right.

NO DOOR-TO-DOOR, NO DEBATE
January 14, 2014

This is always a funny time of the year. We're all coming out of that holiday haze. We're all thinking, "Did that really happen?" Did I use my Visa at a place called Vincent's Tub of Fish and Go-Karts Inc.? And did Canada Post come out and say it was stopping all home delivery in cities?

Yes, yes it did. I remember now—on December 11, the day after the House of Commons closed for Christmas, so nobody could ask the Prime Minister about it. And then the next day, Peter Van Loan came out and suggested that anyone who lived in a city and got home delivery was basically a spoilt rich person, unlike hard-working rural Canadians. Is there any issue in this country that our government can't deal with by pitting Canadians against one another?

And then the head of Canada Post, when he was asked how this would affect people in cities who are seniors and disabled and don't drive cars, said without irony that seniors like to remain active, so this will force them to exercise. There's Canada's problem in a nutshell right there: lazy seniors. Look at the weather we've been having this past month. Now let's round up all the seniors every morning, throw 'em outside, march 'em to a supermailbox and a kilometre back, see who makes it. Survival of the fittest. *There's* an action plan.

Maybe I'm wrong. Maybe these supermailboxes will be good for seniors and the disabled; they'll start to resemble those shrines we see at Lourdes or St. Joseph's Oratory in Montreal. Next to each supermailbox, frozen in the ice will be piles of crutches, scooters and walkers belonging to those who have been cured—or perished.

What I want to know is: Where is the debate in this country? Where is the discussion? This involves five million households. What are the options? What about home delivery three days a week? What about home delivery just for the seniors and just for the disabled? The customer is always right, but the owner calls the shots. In this case, Canadians, we're both. We deserve to be consulted.

GIVE THE GIFT OF GOAT

December 3, 2013

Here we are, in the month of December, heading into Christmas—a season of reflection, a season of giving. And boy, do we give, which is a good thing. Half of our economy is built on the notion that we all max out our credit cards in December, purchasing things that will be broken or discarded by February 9. But for many people that's what the season is all about. It gives us great joy to give gifts to the people we love, especially the children.

But then there's the flip side, the madness of the season. Things like the Secret Santa office pool—which, I'm sorry, I'm just gonna say it, does not bring joy to anyone. It's the opposite. It brings anguish, resentment and regifting. If you are a grown man or woman, there is nothing you need at the dollar store for under ten dollars. Oh look, it's um . . . it's a mug.

If you were born in Canada, if you live in Canada, you won the lotto. Which is why, this Christmas, my sister is not getting an iTunes gift card, she's getting a goat from Plan Canada for seventy-five bucks. Now, she doesn't keep the goat—the goat goes to a family in Africa—but you get the idea. And if that's out of your budget, they also do sheep for fifty bucks. Chickens are available, as are vaccines. And my personal favourite, the ten-dollar anti-malaria bed net—a perfect stocking stuffer.

This season, tell them you love them with Plan Canada— and do it with a goat.

NOVEMBER RAIN

November 26, 2013

The RCMP has finally confirmed it is investigating the Prime Minister's Office for criminal wrongdoing. No surprise, really; the entire operation stinks like day-old mussels. But what I find truly astounding is that until recently, the Prime Minister himself denied over and over again that any investigation was happening. In fact, when it was suggested, he stacked one high horse on top of another high horse, crawled up on top and did a handstand of indignation.

This reminds me of many years ago. I walked out my front door in Newfoundland into a torrential rainstorm. It was freezing cold. There was a neighbour standing in the middle of the street in a T-shirt. I knew something was wrong. I said to him, "You have to go indoors. It's raining out." He looked at me, perfectly calm, and said, "If I say it's not raining, it's not raining." Turns out he was having a full-blown psychotic episode. It happens.

What's the Prime Minister's excuse? His chief of staff wrote a cheque to a senator for ninety thousand dollars. The RCMP says that's bribery. The Prime Minister went into the House of Commons and said, "Nobody in my office knew." We now know a lot of them knew.

So if you believe our Prime Minister, these people who knew either hid it from Stephen Harper or lied to Stephen Harper. Either way, they allowed Stephen Harper to mislead the country. Well, when Stephen Harper found out about this, what did he do? Did he fire these people? No. Two of them got promotions. One of them is now his new chief of staff, the same job that Nigel Wright had when he wrote the cheque. Who does that? I'll tell you who: someone who doesn't know when it's raining, or someone who's been in on it all along.

Jann Arden,
My Very Special Guest

JANN ARDEN IS A DEAR FRIEND who refuses to take my calls.

Or at least that's what she would like you to think.

Jann Arden was my most frequent regular guest on a show that did not have regular guests.

The popularity of Jann's appearances on the show cannot be understated. Not a day goes by when someone doesn't tell me how much they love Jann. Not a day goes by when someone does not admonish me for scaring her all the time or tell me we should just get married already. (There is one obvious reason why that marriage would never work. She is in love with her dog, Midi.)

My relationship with Jann started, appropriately, in her hometown of Calgary, Alberta. I don't remember the exact circumstances that led me to call the future Mrs. Mercer, but I remember it was a day when everything had gone to hell.

For a show like ours, it is a miracle that this didn't happen more often. The strength of our show, four people travelling quickly, all over Canada, was also our unspoken weakness. We operated with no safety net. We would air segments within days of shooting them. This is simply not done in television. News operates that way, but prime-time shows shot on location don't. I loved the adrenaline rush of such a tight schedule.

Unfortunately, on occasion, despite all best efforts, we would show up at a location and find out that the event we had planned on attending was not exactly as advertised.

ME: Hello, we were under the impression that there would be two hundred people here, rolling down a hill in barrels, and that there was going to be a giant foam pit, and there would be Olympians.

FRIENDLY LOCAL: Oh, you must have been talking to Jerome. He was in charge of that.

ME: Yes, that's our contact—Jerome.

FRIENDLY LOCAL: He had a breakdown. He's in Arizona now, resting. He's also up on charges for embezzling.

ME: So there are no Olympians here?

FRIENDLY LOCAL: No. But there's a lady in town with a wiener dog that's half-paralyzed and drags himself around by his front paws in a little wheelchair. That would be funny on your show.

Weather was also a constant battle. The logistics of getting from A to B and then on to C in the winter in Canada is always a challenge. When you are on a tight production schedule, praying that flights won't be grounded or that the weather will cooperate is madness, but that is exactly how we operated. There was no other way to do it.

We actually had a tremendous batting average. The weather gods were kind to us more often than not, and thanks to a crack producer by the name of Tom Stanley, 99 percent of the time when I arrived somewhere, everything was in place and ready to shoot.

So I don't remember the details of that particular day. I just remember that I was in Calgary and whatever shoot we had planned had disappeared. There was no time to regroup, to change cities or reschedule another shoot, so we were on our own. It was the worst-case scenario.

I would, when feeling cocky, often brag that if worse came to worst I could take a camera anywhere in Canada and find a story. This was a day when that boast would be put to the test. Unfortunately, I had a nagging suspicion that the story that I would find was that people in Calgary were in a rush to get to work and not eager to talk. Scintillating television.

I toyed with the notion of doing a tour of Calgary, but it's not my town. To make it credible I would need a tour guide, someone who loved Calgary and who could, on a moment's notice, show me why.

Enter Jann Arden.

As luck would have it, she was in the city and at home. This, I have since discovered, is an extremely rare occurrence. Jann works like a Torbay pony. She does not stop. She is constantly touring.

I tracked down a number.

"Hi Jann, it's Rick Mercer calling. Want to do my show? Maybe show me around Calgary?"

"I could do that," she said. "When are you thinking? I go on tour in a week, then I'm in Nashville, then recording in Vancouver, then I'm shooting a pilot, then I'm—"

"I was thinking today would be good . . . like in an hour?"

"Cripes—give a girl time to shower! Where are you?"

And just like that—no agent, no deal, no nothing—Jann showed up one hour later at my hotel, driving herself, no makeup, hair akimbo, ready to go.

"This will be easy," she said. "Calgary is amazing." She had lots of ideas on how to show off her town. "We can go to Olympic Park, we can go to the zoo . . ."

I had to interrupt. After all, I was the TV professional. I explained to her that while that all sounded great, there was no way we could just show up at a zoo or the Olympic Park and expect access without contacting the proper people and getting permission from God knows what kind of bureaucracy.

Not for the last time, she looked at me with a combination of pity and confusion.

"Don't be ridiculous. Of course they will. Let's go!"

I don't know if I spoke another word that day. I know I laughed for hours, and at the end of it we had enough material for three segments.

And true to her word, there was no such thing as a closed door for her in Calgary. Jann Arden's got all the keys.

At the zoo they not only let us come in, but they gave us the run of the place. They passed me the shovel and introduced me to the elephants.

At Olympic Park they welcomed us with open arms and allowed me to strap Jann to a luge and send her down the icy track.

And she went for it.

As her screams reverberated over the historic hill, I knew that I had found my spirit animal.

Moments before she took the plunge down the luge track, 127

she looked into the camera and said, "Never go on a date that requires you to wear a helmet."

I made a silent promise that it would not be our last.

And so it began.

Over the years I dangled Jann from the top of the CN Tower and sent her down the world's fastest zip line. We shot paintballs at each other. I catapulted her into the foam pit at Kyle Shewfelt Gymnastics, and I put her on the back of a Brahman bull. I love to hear that lady scream.

Throughout it all a real friendship evolved.

Together we hosted the Canadian Country Music Association Awards. Even there, I made her wear a helmet and a harness.

These days, faced with the prospect of no TV show to bring us together, we have started appearing live. We are very creative people and so we call our show "An evening with Jann and Rick." We have performed at fundraisers for the Calgary Health Trust and in Toronto for Casey House, a hospice for people living with HIV/AIDS. It's something we both hope to continue doing well into our old age.

Jann is 100 percent authentic. She is not a diva. She has no self-censor. She loves Calgary and Alberta with every fibre of her being. She is a proud Canadian. Her mouth and her Twitter feed get her in no end of trouble, and I love her for it.

Over the years she always said yes to our dates, and she has only bailed on me once. It's a shame because I had such high hopes for the segment.

I was invited to explore a giant cave filled with a few hundred thousand bats.

Of course I thought of Jann.

As I explained to her, it would be a piece of cake. A helicopter would drop us at the top of a mountain and we would stroll into a cave filled with a million tonnes of bat poo—and live bats would get stuck in her hair.

You don't have to be a genius to know that would be good TV. Plus there would be the educational aspect: we would learn about these unfairly maligned creatures, about their importance to the ecosystem—and again, bats would get stuck in Jann's hair.

I could hear the screams echoing off the mountains as I pitched it to her. I told her she would be 100 percent safe.

And Jann, of course, agreed.

Now, an avid viewer may wonder why they don't remember this segment.

It is because everything went terribly wrong.

Jann was the first casualty. We had to reschedule our descent into the cave owing to the mating patterns of horny bats. This delay put the shoot in the middle of one of Jann's tours and she simply couldn't make it.

I'm sure she was devastated.

I know I was. I knew the show was coming to a close and thought it would probably be our last segment together. I figured it was a surefire winner. That said, we were undeterred and proceeded with the shoot without Jann.

It wasn't that complicated. A small-plane flight to a remote area and then a short helicopter ride to the top of a mountain, where we would meet up with some bat experts. It was the kind of adventure the crew of the *Mercer Report* loved.

I remember being uneasy in the small plane. We were rocking and rolling the entire way. None of us on the crew were nervous flyers, but nobody likes being tossed around in a five-seater plane over mountains. It's unsettling at best. We dealt with these situations the way we always did: any time the four of us boarded a small charter for a show business adventure in dodgy weather, it was inevitable that someone hummed "La Bamba" or mentioned Buddy Holly.

Of course, as always, the plane landed without incident. We felt like rock stars as we transferred to our chartered helicopter on the tarmac.

Helicopters are the ultimate toy. Over the years we relied on them many times to get to a place that would otherwise be impossible to reach. Some of our greatest collective memories as a crew involve helicopter flights over incredible scenery, up riverbeds, over wildlife, through fiords or over glaciers, and today it would be to a mountaintop. The only difference on this day was that Don Spence would not be dangling out the side with his camera on his shoulder. We were simply passengers getting from A to B. The segment would start on the mountaintop.

Usually, a chopper ride is quite enjoyable and relaxed. This time, it was neither of those things. The wind never let up. On occasion it felt like the helicopter was dropping fifty or sixty feet at a time, only to be suddenly thrown twice as high. Occasionally we found ourselves travelling sideways. The pilot responded by putting the nose down and moving forward at a forty-five-degree angle.

When we approached the mountaintop for an initial circle over the landing site, we all had the same reaction. We did not see anything that remotely looked like a landing pad. We saw a small ledge on a mountain, and only that. From the air it looked like it barely had room for us passengers, let alone the helicopter.

But this pilot knew the area well; he had landed on that

spot many times. He knew exactly what he was doing. Still, all of us sensed that this was different than any other flight we had been on. For the first time in a decade, I felt motion sick.

All I could think of was how glad I was that Jann was on tour and playing a show in a soft-seat theatre. We had had a lot of fun over the years, but the reality is I always knew everything we were doing was entirely safe. Anything scary was "TV scary." What was happening now was legitimately terrifying.

The pilot told us we would have one shot and one shot only, and this would not be a regular landing. We were going to attempt a "hot off-load": he was going to hover inches off the ground and we would jump off the chopper onto the ledge with all our gear. We would shut the door behind us and hit the dirt and he would take off immediately.

I could only imagine what would come out of Jann's mouth if she were told we would be executing a "hot off-load."

Don and I shared a look. I was sitting in the back of the chopper, facing the front. Don was in front of me, but we were face to face as we went in for the landing.

Suddenly, I felt the wind take the chopper. Our speed increased. We were no longer over the landing spot. We were headed directly towards what I could see was the side of a cliff.

An alarm, which I later learned was a "ground proximity warning," started to wail. Except it wasn't the ground that we were close to, it was a rock wall.

There have only been a few moments in my life when I felt like I was about to die, and this one is at the top of the list.

I thought, "And this is where it comes to an end."

I could see the cliff face looming in the near distance. Don, with his back to the mountain, was entirely oblivious. Should

I tell him? Should I point? Should I scream?

I decided there was no point. Why tell a guy he's about to bite it? I shut my eyes.

It crossed my mind that it was bad enough that we were all about to hit a mountain, but if Jann had been with us, the next day everyone in the country would be saying, "Well, you knew *that* was going to happen."

In that instant, the chopper made a noise that I had never heard before, a high, screaming pitch, and suddenly we were rocketing upwards. We kept going. Up and up, and then sideways. The mountain disappeared.

The alarm stopped.

And we were informed calmly that we were "going down." It was exactly like in the movies.

Except we didn't crash. We landed. Hard. On the ground. The real ground. It was a successful emergency landing. Four hard bumps and a slide to the left, and we came to a stop.

"Well, let's never do that again."

I don't know if four men have ever exited a helicopter at quite that speed before. We didn't even stop to kiss the pilot, but I know we all wanted to.

After a round of hysterical laughter and a spot check for dry pants, we looked around and took stock of where we were. I have never seen anything quite like it. The earth was black and we were next to a giant road. In the distance we could see a truck coming. John, being the producer, started towards the road with plans to flag the thing down.

As it approached, something became clear. This truck was not a regular truck. It was the size of fifteen trucks. It was three bungalows high and two bungalows long. We had landed in what we figured out was a mining operation.

Two other vehicles approached with lights flashing. White king-cab pickups. Out popped a few people, men and women, in orange vests. They took one look at the helicopter and the four of us—and more important, Don's TV camera—and all hell broke loose. We were on private property! This was a no-landing zone! Strictly prohibited! We were to surrender the camera.

Things escalated but then simmered when one of the truck drivers recognized me and figured out who we were. When they first spotted the camera and the chopper, they thought we were some sort of documentary film crew landing where we weren't supposed to be. Gonzo Greenpeace, or Liz May unleashed.

Once it was established that we were not a news crew trying to ambush them but four idiots trying to get to a bat cave in a wind storm on the distant mountain, the truck drivers became as pleasant as one could hope for. As it turns out, private property or no, in an emergency you can land pretty much anything anywhere you want.

They offered us a ride to the distant mountain, where we could hike up a trail for forty minutes to the cave opening. The pilot, for his part, was done for the day. It was getting dark, and he made it clear he would be leaving as soon as possible, and we would be alone. Conditions had deteriorated and he wasn't taking passengers. He would, however, send help when he returned to his base.

For some reason, probably because we all lived by the adage "the show much go on," we took the truck drivers up on their offer of a lift to the trail that would lead us, in the dark, to the mouth of the cave. This was a decision we immediately regretted once the kind truck drivers dropped us off.

One of the women in the orange vests approached Michal Grajewski. "You can't go up there at night without these," she said, passing him four complimentary cans of bear spray. "You have to hold them in your hands the entire time. Never take your finger off the trigger."

Apparently, the secret to using bear spray is that you have to wait until the very last second before you blast them in the eyes and nose. You have to wait until you can feel the bear's breath on your face. Spray too early and it will do nothing to the bear but will blow into your eyes, immediately incapacitating you. You will fall to the ground, blind and gasping for air, leaving the bear with a pre-seasoned Caucasian male to devour.

While watching Michal's face as he dutifully read the instructions on the side of the can, I made an executive decision.

"To hell with bats. Who's up for calling it a day?"

The drive back was memorable for a few reasons. One, we were all grateful to be alive—this band of brothers had dodged the bullet; and two, we stopped on the way, and in the fading sun we observed a giant grizzly bear playing with her cubs fifty feet away from the road.

It was the first and still only time I had seen a grizzly in the wild, a giant, majestic creature, and the babies were as adorable as you can imagine. When the mother looked up and gave us the stink eye, I was very pleased that I was observing from the relative safety of a two-tonne king cab.

It was a beautiful moment.

All I could think was: "I wish Jann were here. She loves animals. She'd enjoy this."

The Calgary Dream Team. I reached out to these folks many times. Mayor Naheed Nenshi, Jann Arden and Olympian Kyle Shewfelt prepare to zip-line at Canada Olympic Park.

That day when rapelling down a waterfall with the Hamilton Police went terribly wrong.

George Chuvalo never went down. I'm like that but I went down in three seconds flat. A new record.

A BROKEN FAITH

November 5, 2013

Prior to the Battle of Vimy Ridge in 1917, Conservative Prime Minister Robert Borden said this to the Canadian men in uniform: "As you go forward into this action, know that your courage is known to the nation and know that no man, whether he comes home or remains in Flanders, shall have cause to reproach the government for having broken faith."

Well, flash forward to 2013. That faith is broken.

Canadian soldiers qualify for a fully indexed pension after ten years of service. And this month, as we head into Remembrance Day, our government has been throwing soldiers out of the service six and seven months shy of that magic ten-year mark because they are no longer technically eligible to deploy overseas.

And why can't they be deployed overseas? Because they are missing limbs; they are blind; they are deaf; they are suffering from post-traumatic stress disorder. We sent them to Afghanistan, they came back broken and our government has found a loophole to throw them to the curb, so no pension for them.

How does a government allow this to happen? Canada's last three defence ministers promised over and over again that this would never happen. They should all take off their poppies and stab themselves in the head. Cabinet ministers, by the way, like all MPs, qualify for their fully indexed pensions after six years on the job. Not that being a cabinet minister is not a dangerous job. Most of them gain two suit sizes for every year they serve. The threat of adult-onset diabetes is real.

But this goes beyond politics. How we treat injured veterans goes to the very heart of what we stand for as a nation. We ask these men and woman to defend us; if we harm them, when they can no longer defend themselves, we stand for nothing.

ANSWER THE QUESTION—PERIOD

October 29, 2013

L ast week was one of those rare weeks when everyone was suddenly paying attention to the goings-on in Ottawa. And from a showbiz perspective, the House of Commons had it all: scandal, betrayal, intrigue. The only thing missing was gratuitous nudity. And I was thinking that the Prime Minister, the government, the MPs must be stoked because they know that, for the first time in a long time, people are paying attention. They are going to bring their A game.

No such luck.

It's like they all got together and decided to intentionally ensure nobody would watch ever again. It's called Question Period. MPs get to stand up and ask the government questions, and they're supposed to get answers. It's there because we decided a long time ago it's an improvement over sword fights and duelling. But it is broken and it needs to be fixed.

How about from now on, if someone asks the Prime Minister a question like, I don't know, say, "Prime Minister, when you said that nobody in your office was aware of the secret payment to the senator, were you telling the truth? Yes or no?" he's got to answer the question. If he doesn't answer or he stands up and starts talking about trade deals, a giant red X appears on the screen and a buzzer goes off. I know, it's not very elegant, but it's better than the system we have now. Now, when the Prime Minister avoids a question, his caucus leaps to their feet and they start cheering like little girls at a Justin Bieber mall appearance.

Normally I bemoan the fact that young people don't pay attention to politics, but you know, maybe it's a good thing, because really, parliamentarians, you are a bad example to youth. If it's not acceptable at the dinner table, why is it acceptable at the House of Commons?

I don't care what party's in power or who the Prime Minister is. When you have a leader of a party that refuses to provide a straight answer to a straight question about something that happened on their watch, then it's time for that party to find a leader who will.

FREE STAFF

October 22, 2013

Don't be alarmed, but they are everywhere. They walk among us. You go into any place of employment in this country, and they look like employees, they sound like employees, they've got the nametag or the clipboard or the construction boots or the shovel. They are the unpaid interns; young people working for free.

Working for free, by the way, is supposed to be against the law. Or it used to be. Now it's all part of the new economic reality. The reality being that youth unemployment in this country is somewhere around 15 percent. People are desperate. I can't tell you how many emails I've received from friends or friends of friends saying, "Please, please hire my son or daughter to work in your office as an intern. They will do anything. You don't have to pay them. You can work them until they fall asleep in their soup—if you let them have soup."

You have to admit, from an employer's perspective it's a pretty good deal. And as an added bonus, unpaid interns aren't covered under any health or safety laws. So they're not even like people; they're more like a shrub or a plant. Yes, one hopes the plant gets water and sunlight, but there's no law that says you have to take care of the cactus.

Now, all internships are not created equal. There are excellent programs out there where the interns are paid a stipend and the experience is invaluable. The Prime Minister's Office has paid interns. A couple of months ago they were all sent out to crash a Justin Trudeau press conference and pretend they were protesters and heckle and disrupt, and then they all ran away when someone asked where they work. For a young person interested in politics, that kind of experience is invaluable. If you thrive in that atmosphere, you could be offered full-time work.

But the unpaid internship? It's a bad road. And it flies in the face of capitalist principles. You ask any one of them. You give a guy something for free, they will not respect it. The "free" in "free market" should not refer to the staff.

OUTBREAK

October 15, 2013

It seems like yesterday that I was walking in this alley, talking about the state of the Canadian Senate. But in fact, it was many months ago. Canada was a far more innocent place back then. Back then, we were finding out that Senator Mike Duffy, Stephen Harper's favourite fundraiser, did not in fact live on PEI. The RCMP investigated, and it turns out his official residence is somewhere in the Prime Minister's lower colon.

But who could have guessed that once we had pulled on that thread, the Prime Minister's universe could unravel so much.

Senator Pam Wallin, another favourite, has been spending so much time billing taxpayers for personal airline travel, not only is she not officially a resident of Saskatchewan—she's not technically a resident of Earth.

The Prime Minister's chief of staff resigns in disgrace.

The Prime Minister's former Parliamentary secretary, Dean Del Mastro, charged with election fraud.

Patrick Brazeau, Carolyn Stewart Olsen. The alley is not long enough to keep going.

But I was thinking: The Prime Minister appointed every one of these people. It should be statistically impossible to appoint that many train wrecks. Serious question: Has anyone checked the Prime Minister's office for lead pipes? Because it's like everyone close to that man has brain damage. Their moral compass has been destroyed. I'm mostly worried that it could be contagious, because if it is airborne, we are in serious trouble. Can you imagine if regular citizens started acting like these people? All hell would break loose. Suddenly people would start stealing from their employers and their churches, and they would become convinced that the normal rules do not apply to them. Red lights and green lights would be meaningless.

Normally when a group of people start to exhibit bizarre symptoms in a cluster, health officials are called in. So never mind the RCMP—it's time for a quarantine.

TAXATION WITHOUT REPRESENTATION
October 8, 2013

The United States and Canada: two great countries, great friends. But more important, combined we are the largest democratic land mass in the entire world. So it is interesting to note that the government of the United States can cease to function at the drop of a hat and here in Canada we are once again prorogued.

Now, of course, things aren't as bad up here as they are down there. When our Parliament is prorogued, the mechanics of government still work: taxes are collected, the mail is delivered, veterans are abused on a daily basis. But MPs do not sit in the House of Commons, so nobody can ask the government a question. And I mean nobody. Even reporters can't ask questions anymore. I looked into it, and compared to other world leaders, Hugo Chávez has answered more questions from the press than Stephen Harper in the last six months—and Chávez died seven months ago.

When MPs go back to work next week—if Harper lets them go back—they will have gone 117 days without sitting in the House of Commons. There's a word for people on that schedule: unemployed. The difference being, MPs are still paid, which is why you don't hear any bleating from the backbench. They love the notion of representing their constituents from the privacy of their basement or their bass boat.

This is our fault. We have all become comfortable with a system where the Prime Minister can simply close Parliament on a whim. There's a term for that; it's called "taxation without representation." In the United States it led to the American Revolution. In Canada it's becoming business as usual.

Democracy takes practice. We either use it or lose it.

A MAN OF THE PANDAS

April 2, 2013

Sir Wilfrid Laurier once quipped that the twentieth century would belong to Canada. Not quite. But by the looks of it the twenty-first century may be ours because, thanks to Stephen Harper, our country—Canada, the true north strong and free—has pandas.

And not just any pandas—giant pandas from China.

Well, they're not *our* pandas exactly. They're rental pandas. But at ten million bucks, they are awesome. And I for one am proud to be on the panda train. Kudos to our Prime Minister for clearing his schedule, gassing up the plane and flying to Toronto to meet the pandas in person. He's only done that previously for President Obama and the Queen. And this is way cooler because, unlike those two, there's a chance the pandas will mate on Canadian soil.

What an honour it must have been for the pandas themselves. I mean, think of it: one minute you're sitting there in Chengdu, chewing on a bamboo shoot spiked with benzodiazepine, and fifteen hours later you wake up on the tarmac at Pearson International, where Stephen Harper is banging on your cage and making a smiley face. These are moments in a panda's life that they will not forget.

Kudos also to my friends at the CBC News Network for their exhaustive coverage. I'm too young to remember the moon landing or the end of the Second World War, so it's nice to know what witnessing those events must have felt like.

Don't get me wrong. I've always had a soft spot for big, cuddly vegetarians that purr when a prime minister scratches them behind the ear. But enough about John Baird. Stephen Harper said that over the coming years, thanks to these pandas, we will learn more about one another and ourselves— namely, we can forget federal responsibility for national debt, youth unemployment or the sorry state of Aboriginal schools, because . . . We got pandas!

I am ashamed to admit that I did something this week that I promised myself I would never do again. Five years after going cold turkey, I fell off the wagon. I found myself in the nation's capital, I had a few hours to kill, I let down my guard, and the next thing you know I was in the House of Commons, sitting in the gallery, watching Question Period live.

Why do I do this to myself? Like so many addicts, I believed enough time had passed since I gave up the habit. "I can go to one," I thought. "What harm will one do? It will be great!"

No such luck. I was left feeling angry, bitter, depressed and empty on the inside. And that was just the first five minutes. In fact, the only thing that had changed since the last time I was there is that there were no children present, which is a good thing. I want young people in this country to grow up believing that serving in Parliament is an honourable thing to do. As it stands now, going to Question Period live is like attending one of those "Scared Straight" programs where kids are dragged into maximum-security prisons to be freaked out by big gang members.

It's not pretty. I mean, the place is filled with not very nice people who have nothing to lose because they could never survive in the outside world. Their behaviour is completely unacceptable in a civilized society. And I'm talking about the House of Commons now, not a federal prison.

MPs from all parties love to say they believe in transparency. And yet, when you attend Question Period live, where the nation's business is being conducted on the public's dime, the first thing that happens is they confiscate your cell phone. They do this not because they don't want you talking on your cell phone, but because they're terrified someone might roll video to show people on the outside what's really going on. In fact, keeping us in the dark is the only thing all the parties actually agree on, which is reason number one for that to change.

SCIENCE IN SILENCE

February 26, 2013

Another week, another story about scientists in Canada being muzzled. This time it's eggheads in the Arctic studying climate change—a joint project between the Canadians and the Americans. And of course our government told them they had to sign a piece of paper saying they could never discuss their findings in public unless a political staffer in Ottawa said it was okay, which is never going to happen.

The Canadians, of course, did what they were told and signed on the dotted line. Because, well, they want to eat. But the American scientists went ballistic because, well, they're Americans and you know what the Americans are like. It's "freedom of speech this" and "freedom of speech that." And the way they were carrying on, you'd swear that they had been transported back in time and dropped behind the Berlin Wall at the height of the Cold War. Nope, you're in Canada in 2013. You want to do science in these parts, you'd better get used to it.

And get over yourselves. It's not like scientists are the only ones in this country being told to shut up. It's everyone. Remember when Canada used to have a Veterans Affairs Ombudsman? He appeared on television every night and screamed bloody murder whenever the government abused our veterans. Well, he's gone. They've got a new guy now. Do a Google news search and he barely comes up.

Then there's the cabinet. If scientists have been muzzled, half the cabinet have had their voice boxes removed. And as for the backbenchers, they've taken to communicating with a series of blinks and twitches like in a hostage video.

So if you're a scientist, don't take it personally. Times have changed. The days are over when you could discuss your findings in public. It is a bygone era, like smoking in the supermarket. This is the new Canada: Thank you for not talking.

CASH CRISIS

January 15, 2013

Two rules I like to live by: 1) Never discuss money in public—it's tacky; 2) Try to avoid stating in public that someone or something is stupid. It's rude. It lacks wit.

That said, our new money—the plastic bills—are stupid. I can't think of another word for it. I have no idea what they were thinking. Somewhere in Ottawa, someone in government said to someone else in government, "We have a new plan for money. It will make it harder to counterfeit and last longer." "Well, that's great news. Is there a downside?" "No, no, there's no downside . . . oh, except you can't fold this money in half, but that's okay. Canadians will just have to carry clutch purses like Nan used to have. Also, the bills stick together. So if your bar tab is thirty-seven bucks and you give the guy forty and say keep the change, you might give him your rent money without knowing it. Also, if you reach into your pants for your car keys, when your hand comes out the money tends to fly away, but that's great because the polymer bills have the magical flight properties of miniature hand gliders."

I'm not against progress, but this is progress run amok. I only hope that someday we will look back and say, "Do you remember when Pop Shoppe was going to put Coca-Cola out of business? And do you remember those rain jackets that you could ball up and carry around in a pouch on a stylish belt? And do you remember when we had plastic money? Boy, that was stupid. Thank God those days are over."

No such luck. We are powerless here. It's not like you can boycott money. The future is here and it is plastic. And sadly, there's no cure for stupid.

BEST SHOT

November 27, 2012

The malls are packed and the bells are jingling. It's that wonderful time of year when Canadians from all walks of life prepare to experience the miracle of flu season. There hasn't been a lot of talk about the flu this year. We only get freaked out when the name has something to do with pigs or chickens. Yet every year the old-fashioned no-name flu kills a whack of Canadians—basically, the population of Flin Flon. (Good town.) And the best defence, better than washing your hands or even avoiding that moron who comes to work sick and then coughs on your neck in the elevator, is the flu shot.

In my office we gave it away for free. I stood there and said, "Okay, folks: free flu shot. Who's in?" Two out of ten people made a move—*two out of ten*. If I had said there were free smoked-meat sandwiches at the end of the hall, there would have been a stampede. Turns out a lot of people won't get the flu shot on principle. Why? Well, "I haven't had the flu in years, why would I get a flu shot?" said one. Good point. I have never been run over by a car, so why would I look both ways? My favourite is when someone looks at you very seriously and says, "Did you know there's dead flu virus in the flu vaccine?" Yes, I am aware of that. It's why it's called a vaccine. It's why we don't all have polio.

I have one friend who refuses any vaccines at all based on something he read on the internet. But to be fair, he still smokes Export "A" in the green package, so he's basically a medical doctor.

Look, I get lazy. *I'm* lazy. I get afraid of needles. But even if you are healthy enough to fight the flu, if you get the flu, chances are you could pass it on to someone who can't fight it. So come on, Canada, roll up your sleeve. It's just a little prick. Don't be one, get one.

APPS FOR HEROES

November 13, 2012

As all Canadians know, there's nothing more moving than watching veterans of the Second World War or Korea attend a Remembrance Day ceremony.

Those people have been there my entire life. As time marches on, Canada loses five hundred veterans each week. But they're not gone yet. There are over 100,000 of them still alive and living in Canada—a fact that is lost on the federal government. In the last budget, the finance minister said cuts wouldn't affect people, that they were backroom cuts. That's a bit of a stretch—especially if you consider veterans to be people.

This year alone, Veterans Affairs is going to close nine offices across Canada. So if you're a veteran and you have a problem, what do you do? Well, you don't go into an office and talk to a real person—those days are over. There's a 1-800 number you can call.

Or—and this is my favourite, bearing in mind that their average age is eighty-eight—there's an app veterans can download to their smart phones that will allow them to navigate the Veterans Affairs website. A website that will send them to the nearest Service Canada office, where, if they need to make burial arrangements, they have to take a number and stand in line behind some guy like me who's waiting to get his passport renewed.

If you fought on the beach in Dieppe and survived, you should not have to spend any portion of your final days on this Earth in a Service Canada office. The fact that a majority of our MPs voted to send those who served on the front lines to the back of the line means "lest we forget" is meaningless. Clearly, we've forgotten.

WHO NEEDS FRESH WATER?

October 30, 2012

It has been suggested that the Harper government, previously known as the Government of Canada, dislikes science. I never really bought into that, but I'm starting to come around. I figure they can't be against *all* scientists, though—just scientists who study things that don't matter, like water. Case in point: the Experimental Lakes research facility.

If you haven't heard of it, why would you? It's basically seventeen government scientists operating a living laboratory that encompasses fifty-eight freshwater lakes. The work may not sound very sexy, but in the world of science these people are rock stars, renowned the world over.

They're up there, living in tents and shacks, with their big, bushy beards, eating mung beans out of Mason jars, trying to figure out what different chemicals will do to our drinking water. They're the people who figured out the acid rain problem. And now the Harper government is closing them down to save money. How much money? Two million dollars a year.

But here's the kicker: It will cost fifty million to shut them down. Wow! Someone really doesn't like fresh water.

Now, I admit I am biased here. In the interest of full disclosure, let me admit here that I'm a drinker. I drink water at home and work. Heck, I put it in my coffee.

But to me this goes to the very heart of who we are. When I think about what makes Canada great, fresh water is right at the top of the list. We have over two million lakes in this country, and more than enough people who are willing to mess with them.

My Canada includes weird scientists who are devoted to keeping our water clean. When we stand up and we sing "O Canada," we pledge to stand on guard for thee. If that doesn't include our water, we might as well sit down and give up.

LIKE IT'S 2009

October 16, 2012

Lately I've been having this recurring dream. I fall asleep on the couch in front of the TV, and suddenly it's 2009 again. Michael Jackson is about to embark on a world tour. Helena Guergis is a star cabinet minister. The government has launched Canada's Economic Action Plan to stimulate the economy.

I can't be the only one who thinks it's 2009 again. Suddenly every TV show broadcast in Canada is brought to you by Canada's Economic Action Plan. Which is strange, because it's over. It's done. That stimulus thing—it happened—but it's in the past. And yet the Harper government, in this period of austerity, has announced it's going to spend sixteen million dollars on brand-new Economic Action Plan ads. Why? Deep in their hearts, they must think we're very stupid. They think we won't care that they're cutting prison chaplains and meat inspection and scientists, not when this week's episode of *Glee* or *Honey Boo Boo* is brought to us by Canada's Action Plan. "Hey look, Pa! They're doing stuff!" And they must think the ads are going to make us feel good, like those touchy-feely Church of Latter-day Saints ads used to make us feel back in 2009.

Look, I get it. Governments are always going to spend money on priorities that some of us don't like. But does anyone think it's a good idea to spend money advertising something that doesn't exist? Show me someone who thinks that's a good idea and I'll show you someone who needs a CAT scan.

Card sharks have one technique in common. They distract you with one hand so you have no idea what the other hand is doing. And at sixteen million dollars in advertising, that is one expensive hand. Don't fall for it.

WHERE'S THE BEEF FROM?

October 9, 2012

The thing that freaks me out the most about this whole meat recall story is that one processing plant is responsible for a third of the beef products in a country of thirty-five million people.

XL Foods is not just a meat processing plant; it's practically its own country. I'm surprised it doesn't have a seat at the United Nations. Every day, five thousand cows go in one door and come out the other door on Styrofoam trays. But don't worry, there are forty meat inspectors working two shifts, which means they inspect three and a half cows every sixty seconds. So, no blinking!

Does anyone think this is a good idea? I know the minister of agriculture thinks it's a good idea—but does anyone on this planet agree with him? And here's a question: Who the hell are XL Foods? If you go to their website, you will see that they are a company that is "built on trust and a firm handshake." Past that, it's all a mystery. It's all pictures of cows grazing in meadows. It's like a website for a spa. And then, way down in the corner, there's a button labelled RECALL INFORMATION.

It's like a secret society. It took weeks for people to figure out who owned the company. Combine that with a minister of agriculture who spends half his time in witness protection and we might as well all just crawl into a freezer and shut the door.

This is not a meat recall, it's a wake-up call. The entire system is designed to keep us in the dark. If we let it stay that way, we're cooked.

WORKING HARD FOR A NON-LIVING

October 2, 2012

'm very happy to hear that Air Canada is creating 1,100 new jobs. This is good news for our country, because as everyone knows, a job at Air Canada—that's a good job. In fact, some people would say too good. After all, the Conservative government twice had to table back-to-work legislation to keep Air Canada employees in line. Apparently, they're a little bit greedy.

But the legislation worked. Once the union was put in its place, lo and behold, there was prosperity. One thousand, one hundred new jobs.

Except it turns out they are not full-time jobs. A buddy of mine who lives in Ottawa and is looking for work sent me the job listing. They're permanent part-time jobs—minimum twenty hours a week, maximum thirty-two hours a week, no more. You have to work sliding shifts, on weekends and holidays, and you have to be able to lift seventy pounds over and over again. Preference is given to bilingual candidates. But hey, union job, thirty-two hours a week—and the pay is $10.80 an hour, a whopping fifty-five cents above minimum wage.

When I worked for minimum wage, I was a dishwasher at the Continental Café. I operated a Maytag. The Air Canada employees will be operating the trucks that drag the two-hundred-million-dollar airplanes around. And as a dishwasher I got a piece of the tips. When was the last time anyone tipped a guy out on the tarmac when it's thirty-two below?

This is a fundamental shift in our country. Welcome to the new discount Canada, where people who work hard for a living can't make a living at all.

WE NEED MORE SCHOOLS LIKE THIS

April 3, 2012

It's a very long time since I've been in school. And like a lot of Canadians, when I see a yellow bus, I breathe into a paper bag and then I carry on with my day. But this past week, I went back to school. And why not? Forty-seven schools from across Canada came together and raised a quarter of a million dollars for kids on the other side of the planet. And I know, it was a contest—"Who can raise the most money?" But let's face it: No matter where you go to school, there's always going to be a school that's bigger, nicer, richer, whatever. The kids know this, and yet they still went to work and raised all that money.

Really, what is wrong with kids today? From where I'm standing, not much. And how about the kids at Peterborough Collegiate Vocational School? What a school! Great sports, great science, they got arts up the yazoo. They have an anti-bullying hotline that hasn't been called in eleven months. And still, this year, they were told out of the blue that their school was closing.

You know, in these situations, you have two options. You can do what you're told or you can fight like hell. These kids, they went with the latter, and boy, what a beautiful sight. They fought, they marched, they made the lives of the school board a living hell, and they still went out and raised fifty grand for kids in Africa.

These kids may not be able to vote, but they could teach us all a thing or two about being engaged citizens. In fact, if I could replace the entire federal cabinet with thirty-nine kids from PCVS, I would do it in a heartbeat.

I take that back. I would replace them with *twenty-five* kids. Harper's cabinet is too big as it is.

The president of the student council at PCVS has said they're going to keep fighting because Canada needs more schools like theirs, not one fewer. I tend to agree. I'm just glad they lasted as long as they did. We're all better off because of it.

NEW LOW OF ROBOCALLS

February 28, 2012

I have always loved politics. I love the competition. I love the ideas. I love the brilliance, the pomposity, and the idiocy of some of the great characters who practise the art. And I have always believed it's an art worth practising.

Now, I understand, in Canadian politics the bar is very low. Let's face it: You've got to get on your stomach and crawl to fit under there. But there has always been a little bit of sunshine. There's always been a little bit of light. This past week, I'm not so sure. I'm talking about robocalls.

We now know that, during the last federal election, hundreds of thousands of calls came out of Edmonton to Liberal and NDP voters in eighteen different ridings, claiming they were coming from Elections Canada, lying, sending people to voting booths that didn't exist.

Now, I understand that in politics, there have always been dirty tricks. But this is not some drunks tearing down some posters. This is not even a negative ad campaign. This is big money and technology targeting people who want to vote and trying to physically stop them. We can't have this.

You put ten Canadians in a room, and they will disagree on ten things. Fine. But we have always agreed that voting is a fundamental right. This is not a left or right thing. This is just a thing. If we don't believe in that, what else do we have to believe in?

If stopping people who want to vote from doing so becomes the new normal, we will have hit a new low in the sewer that is Canadian politics. Keep this up, and we'll need a snorkel to get under that bar. Any deeper, and we all drown.

YOU HAVE BEEN WARNED

February 14, 2012

The great thing about living in a modern democracy is that it is always changing. And I've got to hand it to the party in power: Ever since we elected this strong, stable, majority government, we are getting brand-new rights every single day.

Like this past week, the minister of justice, Rob Nicholson, stood up and announced, out of the blue, that if someone comes onto your property and you think they might be there to steal your all-terrain vehicle or catch your car on fire, you have the right to pick up a gun and fire warning shots at them.

Well, thank God that's cleared up. We all know what it's like: You look down the bottom of the driveway, you see someone funny. You don't know what they're up to. They could be a car burner. Now, I don't own an all-terrain vehicle, but I do own a barbecue, and I don't like to brag, but it's pretty nice. So next time someone comes into my yard— warning shot. And that goes for you too, Mr. Knocking-on-My-Door-Looking-for-Twenty-Dollars-for-the-Cystic-Fibrosis-Walk-Just-When-I'm-Sitting-Down-to-Dinner. You could be a car burner—warning shot.

Now, the greatest threat to my life as a city dweller has nothing to do with people stealing my property, and everything to do with some idiot in a four-thousand-pound SUV who does not know how to use a signal light. Be warned: Do that again, cut me off without signalling— warning shot. And while we're at it, people who do not walk in a straight line on the sidewalk, and people who get on an elevator before letting the people inside the elevator off the elevator—warning shots for the lot of you.

Yes, it's a brave new world. The Minister of Justice, Canada's top cop, is saying don't call the cops—fire at will. If you live across the street, you might want to duck.

BECAUSE DAD SAYS SO

January 17, 2012

Democracy is very messy. In fact, on paper, it doesn't even make a heck of a lot of sense. For starters, it involves all of us—and by all of us, I mean the people. And what's worse, that means it involves people's opinions, a situation that only leads to debate. And let's face it: No matter what the issue, for every sensible person on either side, there are two idiots who are addicted to the sound of their own voice. I should know: I'm one of them.

But speaking of debate, I've noticed lately that some of the messy parts of democracy are slowly being done away with. Remember debate? No, neither do I. It's been a while.

For example, a couple of months ago, Stephen Harper decided to change the name of the Canadian Navy to the *Royal* Canadian Navy. There was no debate; he just announced it. Now, personally, I don't care one way or the other, but people in the navy do. Some of them love it, some of them hate it. But the important thing is, nobody asked for their opinion. Who cares what they think? They just serve in the navy. Who cares what we think? We just pay for it. Nope. Dad said, end of story.

And now we have this pipeline business. Now, I realize I should have paid more attention to this a year ago, but like a lot of Canadians, I find it's only showing up on my radar now. And honestly, I don't know if the pipeline is a good idea or a bad idea. But the good news is, I no longer have to look at both sides. None of us does. No, because Dad has made it perfectly clear: There's only one side to this issue. And anyone who thinks otherwise is an enemy of Canada.

159

I've got to say, this is way better than the old days, when we had the burden of being informed citizens on our shoulders. No, now we have a new job: to be seen and not heard. Welcome to Canada 2012. His house, his rules. God save the King.

WAR ON FUN

December 6, 2011

I don't know what's sadder—that this country woke up a few weeks ago and read the story about a school in Toronto banning the use of soccer balls on the playground, or the fact that deep down, none of us was really surprised.

I know I wasn't, because I am familiar with the Vice-Principal Law of Enjoyment, which states that for every instance of a child having fun, there is an equal or slightly more powerful force that exists solely to stop that activity from happening.

And every generation is different. When I was in grade eight, my school banned the Rubik's Cube. Why? Because some kid was wandering down the hall with his head buried in the Rubik's Cube, went headfirst into a door and split his nose open. And I'm sorry, I remember that kid—he was always walking into doors. In fact, if I bumped into him today, I wouldn't recognize him without the nosebleed.

But the school's rationale was "Well, we can't have kids walking around with their heads down," so they banned the cube. Meanwhile, it is because we wandered around with our heads buried in our Rubik's Cubes that my generation can safely navigate through traffic on foot with our heads down while texting on our phones. You could say it saved our lives.

This is a war on fun. And it is a slippery slope. In 2014—and this is a fact—school clubs in Ontario will no longer be able to fundraise by selling chocolate. Only nutritious items. There's your future, Canada: a sad child on your doorstep, trying to sell you a bag of radishes so they can go on a band trip.

Get used to it. Because if you let them take your balls, your freedom is the next to go.

TIME TO CLOSE THE COMMONS

November 29, 2011

Conservative member of Parliament Rob Anders fell asleep last week, live on national television, right in the middle of Question Period. It was on the news a lot, and people found it funny. Meanwhile, in Toronto last year, some dude whose job it was to sell subway tickets took a nap on the job and it was front-page news. People acted like he was history's cruellest monster. It was very telling.

As time marches on, society changes; and with it, traditions die. It's tough, but someone has to say we're closing down the buggy-whip factory, or that's it, the VCR is going in the garbage. No one wants to be the one to stand up and say the emperor has no clothes, so let me: It's time to close the House of Commons—permanently. Let's face it: It's a soap opera, its ratings are in the toilet and, like all soap operas, it's filled with bad actors and nobody knows their names.

The first job of any MP is to hold government accountable for spending our money. They don't do that anymore. MPs approved fifty million dollars for border security. The Prime Minister took the money and built a hockey rink and a gazebo in Muskoka. And nobody cares! Which is fine. The second job of an MP is to debate bills in Parliament. Those days are over. An agriculture bill in Cuba gets more debate than a Canadian crime bill. And nobody cares, which is fine.

But if MPs aren't going to do their jobs and they can't keep their eyes open long enough to pretend they're doing their jobs, why send them to Ottawa? Keep them in their ridings. Let them do something useful, like help someone fill out a passport application.

And for the rest of the country, can we finally acknowledge what everyone in Ottawa knows but no one will say out loud: MPs and cabinet ministers have nothing to do with running this country. This country is run by twenty-three-year-olds who work in the Prime Minister's Office. They decide what bills are passed; they decide what countries we invade. Let them do their job.

And the Prime Minister? Well, he can be CEO or Sun God or whatever he wants to be called. He can wear a gold hat. As long as he comes out on a balcony occasionally, waves, goes back in, does his thing, comes out five years later and stands for re-election. But it's his show and his show only. Let's stop pretending it's anything else but. And on that point—there is no debate.

MAKE IT BETTER NOW

October 25, 2011

Every year in this country, three hundred kids take their own lives. It is a mind-boggling number. And this past week, one of those kids was Jamie Hubley. He was fifteen, he was depressed and he happened to be gay.

And because this is 2011, we don't just read about a kid like Jamie. We can Google him, and then the next thing you know, you're sitting at home watching his videos on YouTube. And he was gay, all right. He was a great, big goofy gay kid singing Lady Gaga on the Internet. And as an adult, you look at that and you go, You know what? That kid's going places. But for some reason, some kids, they looked at that and they attacked. And now he's gone.

And because this story is all too familiar, we know exactly what's going to happen next. Grief counsellors will go into the school, as they should. But what about the old-fashioned assembly? You know, where the cops show up and there's hell to pay and they find out who's responsible. You know, like when the lunchroom is vandalized. Because the kids who bullied this boy, they know who they are. And more importantly, other kids know who they are.

It's no longer good enough for us to tell kids who are different that it's going to get better. We have to make it better *now*. That's every single one of us. Every teacher, every student, every adult has to step up to the plate.

And that's gay adults, too. Because I know gay cops, soldiers, athletes, cabinet ministers—a lot of us do—but the problem is, adults, we don't need role models. Kids do. So if you're gay and you're in public life, I'm sorry, you don't have to run around with a pride flag and bore the hell out of everyone, but you can't be invisible either.

Not anymore. Three hundred kids is three hundred too many.

CELEBRATE SNOW DAYS
February 8, 2011

Lately I've taken to listening to talk radio. I go online and I pop around the country and see what people are getting angry about. And boy, we are an angry bunch. Usually we're angry because someone somewhere is gettin' away with something. But this past week, the anger in this country has been off the charts. And why? Snow days.

Parents in Toronto are having full-blown aneurysms. And I have to ask you: What is wrong with the adults in this country? And who are these people calling in and saying that when they were kids, there was no such thing as snow days? There were snow days in this country in 1864. The only difference is back then the miserable adults who were complaining couldn't call into a radio station.

Cripes, the kids in Toronto have not had a day off because of snow since 1999. You know what that means? That means there's an entire generation of schoolchildren in Canada's largest city who have no idea what it's like to go to bed at night dreading a math test, only to wake up the next morning and find out, as if by some divine intervention, school has been cancelled. And then they head out, hit the toboggan hill all day, come home, eat supper, pass out because they're exhausted, wake up the next day and botch the math test because they didn't study, because it was a snow day.

And when school is cancelled for no real reason because the big snowstorm doesn't come? Even better. Because when it comes to someone getting away with something for nothing, it doesn't get much better than that. So instead of getting angry about snow days, why don't we celebrate them? Why don't we embrace them for exactly what they are: a rite of passage, a part of being Canadian?

The snow day. It should be put on a stamp.

Confessions of a Political Junkie

WHY POLITICS?

It's hard to give a short answer. And it's a question I've been asked for close to thirty years.

For as long as I can remember, politics has been my spectator sport. It has always been my baseball.

Loving politics does not make me a complete outlier. Most Canadians know one or two political junkies. An avid interest in politics is not considered completely unnatural—unlike, say, a man's love of the trombone—but it is considered by many to be somewhat suspicious.

At least, it is considered suspicious to pay attention to politics to an unnatural extent.

Really—what kind of person sits down every day at five o'clock and watches *Power and Politics* on the CBC News Network?

Well, as a TV professional I have seen the data, and I can tell you exactly how many people do that: me and six others, two of whom can't summon the energy to change the channel or the will to live.

Programs that drill down and analyze the goings-on
in the House of Commons simply don't have a lot of viewers—
especially when the competition is so compelling. Both Rogers
and Bell now have aquarium channels. There is a reason why
commercial advertising on political chat shows in Canada is
dominated by the alpaca farmers of Canada and the makers of
the walk-in tub.

If I had to list things that infuriate me, it would be a long
list, but complete disengagement from the political process
would be at the top. I don't expect Canadians to pay attention
to the obsessive degree that I do, but anything other than a
cursory glance would be an improvement.

To be fair, Canadians will pay attention when they feel it
matters: in the lead-up to an election or during a national crisis.
In my lifetime, I remember the entire country being transfixed
by sovereignty referendums in Quebec and, more recently,
Justin Trudeau's wardrobe choices in India. But paying attention
every four years, or during a titillating escapade, is not enough.

Far too many Canadians view their member of Parliament
the same way they view the baking soda in their fridge. Out
of sight and out of mind. When asked, they can answer in the
affirmative—yes, there is a box in there somewhere, and they
may even know the brand, but they honestly couldn't tell you
what shelf it is on, where it is hiding these days or if it's doing
its job. Nothing short of a giant stink will make them investigate
or replace it.

Sadly, there are some members of Parliament who are
entirely fine with this widespread apathy. And there are
political strategists who count on it.

Ask a hundred people what their dream job is and you will
get a hundred different answers. But who among us would
not sign up for a job where, once you are hired, the boss

doesn't pay attention to a single thing you do? That is the job description for members of Parliament when Canadians don't do their part and fail to keep an eye on them. MPs can only be fired by their constituents—we are the boss. But what's the point if we don't hold them accountable?

One of the reasons I love merging the worlds of comedy and politics, why I love satire, is that I know it can, on occasion, convince people to pay a little more attention to politics. Whether the viewer or reader agrees with me or not is secondary. If they are pissed off enough to look into something a little more closely, if only to confirm their belief that I am on the payroll of Big Pharma or an international cabal of anarchists, that works too.

I know that for many people, ignoring politics is not a lifestyle choice, it's just the way they were raised. How could you have an interest in something you were never exposed to in the first place? It's like me and the sport of cricket. I know that gabillions of people on the planet love cricket; they breathe and bleed cricket. But I don't know any of the teams, the players, and I don't know the rules.

I blame my parents for not being more East Indian.

This is why I support the notion of lowering the voting age. Not because I think a sixteen-year-old has far greater insight than anyone else. Science tells us their brains have not finished growing, but I am fine with them voting anyway. If we get 'em while they're young, we might just have them for life.

We know for a fact that people who are physically active as children are more likely to be physically active for life. This is why we are forced, by the state, to go to gym class. We are hoping this exposure to running endless laps while being barked at by a gym teacher will result in a lifelong passion for and love of fitness.

We also agree that it is worth the investment to provide a public education to our children, to expose them to science, literature and the arts. We want well-rounded citizens. We also need the occasional kid to grow up to cure diseases, write great novels and create music that we do not understand. We rely on this.

But a student in this country can get pretty much all the way through school while avoiding civics, current events or even Canadian history.

Ask any kid in grade twelve how much of their eighteen-year-old life has been spent learning about Canada and how Canada actually works. They will tell you: not a heck of a lot. Ask them how much time they spent learning algebra; different answer.

Democracy is paid lip service. Canada is a specialty subject; it's not on the regular curriculum.

Every major brand in the world spends an inordinate amount of time and money trying to hook 'em when they are young. Banks know that if a first-year college student ends up with their credit card, there is a very good chance that student will be a customer for life. Beer companies know this as well. The list goes on and on.

But for some reason, political parties do not really seem interested in engaging new participants. Parties talk a good game about engaging youth, but for the most part it has always been for show. The parties are happy with what they have. As long as more than half of the people show up on Election Day, it is all good.

Imagine if you heard a news report that said, "Roughly 63 percent of the firefighters on duty last night showed up for the fire." That might be cause for alarm. You might even find yourself saying, "Surely we can do better than that."

The problem is that in politics, some people *like* dis-engagement. When Stephen Harper, whom many consider a political and strategic genius, won the leadership of the newly merged Conservative Party of Canada in 2003, he had his work cut out for him. Harper pledged to take this newly formed party from the political wilderness and supplant the Liberal Party as the "natural governing party of Canada." A Herculean task, no doubt.

One of his very first moves in this bid to grow the party was to shrink it. First on the block? The Conservative Youth Federation, a constitutionally enshrined body within the Progressive Conservative Party of Canada. A youth wing active on practically every campus in Canada that was devoted to recruiting more young conservatives to the cause and ensuring that the concerns of youth were heard at the national caucus level and at policy conventions.

Harper strongly advocated getting rid of the organization. Long considered the farm team for the political right in Canada, it was deemed a waste of time and energy.

I was convinced he had made a colossal mistake. In fact, I remember saying, "The man is dead in the water."

A year later he formed his first government and the Liberals were in turmoil.

Harper's road to a majority government was paved not by appealing to the broadest number of Canadians, but by appealing to a select number whom he wooed with speeches at retirement homes and mid-morning appearances at the local Tim Hortons. No stops on campus needed here.

It was a strategy that drew heavily on a playbook created by the owners of a small Canadian insurance start-up in 1993. They announced a business strategy that everyone in the industry thought was absurd and counterintuitive. They announced they would cater only to people over the age of fifty. If you were between eighteen and forty-nine, they would not even take your call. What a ridiculous notion. In just a few years Grey Power Insurance ruled the industry.

Stephen Harper was watching.

And so, yes, while I have seen beyond a shadow of a doubt that gaming disengaged voters and encouraging more disengagement is a legitimate political strategy, I'd like to think there is another way. I *have* to think that. Politics was imprinted on me at a young age. In much the same way that moms and dads put hockey sweaters on two-year-olds in order to ensure that their child will grow up normal, politics for me was always present.

In Newfoundland and Labrador, politics is a little different than it is in the rest of the country. It is in many ways a blood sport. VOCM, the largest private radio station in the province, has a morning call-in show called *Open Line*, these days hosted by Paddy Daly. Pretty much everyone tunes in at some point. There is not a politician in the province who does not monitor every minute of the program. While callers are allowed to discuss whatever they like, provincial politics dominates. There is a reason why. Newfoundland and Labrador has always produced highly theatrical and entertaining politicians. For such a small place we have always punched above our weight when it comes to producing successful white guys who are full of shit and won't shut up. The pendulum swings wildly in the province. I have seen politicians from Newfoundland who were equipped with the finest of minds and the sharpest of tongues. And then there are those whose success baffles me. I've seen brighter lights on small appliances.

Open Line was on in my house daily while I was growing up, and now, thanks to the advent of streaming radio, no matter   171 where I am in the country, I start my day listening to the show. And while the curriculum in Newfoundland schools certainly didn't spend much time on civics, I was lucky enough to have a personal tutor in the subject: my late godfather, Hugh Shea.

As a child I was fascinated by Hugh. He was perhaps my father's best friend and his polar opposite. In my entire life I can count on one hand the number of times I have heard my father swear. But if you tried to count the number of swear words to come out of Hugh's mouth, you would run out of fingers and toes inside of the first sixty seconds. I loved that.

Short and wiry, a shock of black hair, 120 pounds with a smoking habit that put René Lévesque to shame, he ran for the leadership of the provincial Progressive Conservative party in 1971. That didn't work out, but he was elected as a Conservative member of the House of Assembly the following year. It was an historic election, perhaps the most hard fought and bitter in our history, and when the dust settled it was essentially a tie. The government was in turmoil; nobody knew who had the right, or the ability, to govern. Hugh, the newly elected Conservative, sized up the situation and promptly crossed the floor, momentarily giving the governing Liberals the seats they needed to keep the Tories down.

The good news was, on the day that he crossed, his house was not burnt down, as the mob outside was threatening to do. And if it had been, his wife and kids were safe, hiding out at my parents' place in Middle Cove.

Within weeks the government collapsed and Hugh was out. He was from then on a political pariah. Undeterred, Hugh went on to run many times for the Liberals, always in die-hard Conservative ridings, always unsuccessfully. Eventually, he ran for the leadership of the Liberal party but lost to a man named Leo Barry, who at the time was one of the first men in the province to have a perm. That had to have hurt.

Hugh talked politics to me from a very young age. I showed an interest and he talked to me as if my opinion mattered. He told me who the players were, who was right and who was wrong. He would hold court in the corner store he owned, which was called Shea's Rip-Off. On more than one occasion it doubled as a campaign quarters. If you wanted to find the candidate, he was behind the till.

Years later, after the store was closed, I got a job—my first—peeling potatoes at his next venture, a takeout fittingly called Shea's Hamburger Hell. He was, as they say, "local colour."

Political debates would occur nonstop over the counter of Hamburger Hell. A string of political hangers-on and politicians, failed and successful, municipal and provincial, would come through the doors. Everyone had an opinion. Opinions were served hot; the burgers were not. It was an education. And if I threw my two cents' worth into the conversation, it was all good.

One day at Hamburger Hell, a scraggly bunch came in for a brief chat. After which Hugh allowed them to put a poster in his window and some fliers on his counter. The poster and fliers were promoting a benefit concert in aid of Amnesty International.

When they left, I asked him who exactly Amnesty International were—I assumed they were important. Hugh didn't usually allow posters in the window. That much I knew.

As he answered my question he grew more animated. Arms waving, voice rising, he told me that in all the world there was no greater organization than Amnesty International, that they were devoted first and foremost to the protection of human rights and human dignity all over the planet. And that it was hard for me to understand, living in a country as blessed as Canada, but in many parts of the world, people did not enjoy the freedoms we take for granted. And it was our responsibility, the responsibility of all of us who enjoyed these freedoms, to do everything we could to help others gain theirs. This, he said, was the entire reason that Amnesty International existed.

He presented their case to me as if he was presenting it to the United Nations. I was excited to do my part and sign up for the cause. Taking a flier in my hand, I said to my godfather, "Are you member of Amnesty International?"

He said, "For Jesus' sakes, no. They're all cracked."

Hughie could rant. I learned from the best.

Lucky people, and I count myself among them, can often point to one or more teachers who played an important role in their lives. The teachers who opened their eyes to a new subject or gave the right amount of encouragement at the right time. It's often because of these teachers that a person ends up in a particular occupation. I have had a few of those teachers. Mr. Chalker in grade six was one. I made a saucy and inappropriate crack during a lesson of his on the Great Newfoundland Sealing Disaster. I couldn't help myself. It came to me, and before I knew it I was blurting it out loud. I got a laugh from the class, and despite the grim nature of the subject, I didn't get in trouble. Instead, Mr. Chalker said, "That's a good one. I'm going to write that down." And then he added, "Actually, *you* should write that down."

It never occurred to me to write anything down before. So I started writing things down.

In high school, Lois Brown told me I was going to be an actor in a play we were writing. I had no interest in being on stage. I was committed to writing things down, not saying them out loud on stage. She said, "I don't care. You are going to be in it." So I was in it and I haven't stopped since.

It's because of Mr. Chalker and Lois Brown that I ended up doing what I have done for most of my life: writing things down and ranting out loud about politics.

Always politics.

And why politics? Because, despite the fact that perhaps a majority of Canadians are happy to tune the subject out, I cannot think of a more important one.

Yes, I get everything about politics that people find off-putting. Yes, I understand that people get tired of being lied to, tired of being treated like fools.

But still, despite the negatives, nothing matters in quite the same way politics does.

It has always struck me that the laziest "intellectual argument" ever made is "It doesn't matter who I vote for; they are all the same." I would argue it is so lazy it stretches the definitions of both *argument* and *intellectual*. The only argument or statement more ridiculous is "It doesn't matter who wins; they are all the same."

I have never in all my years seen an election for any position, whether it was class president or prime minister, where this was remotely true.

I like to equate the job to that of running a hospital. We have all been in a hospital as a patient, a visitor or a staff member. I find hospitals awe-inspiring. Imagine what it would take to run such a thing. For starters, real lives are at stake. Decisions that are literally about life or death are made daily. Someone has to run this place, to provide direction, to pick the right people to hire the right doctors and nurses. There need to be mechanisms in place to ensure that the labs run correctly and efficiently, that the staff schedules are practical. And then there is the parking!

Next time you are looking at a leaders' debate, ask yourself: "Who would I chose to run the hospital?"

They won't have to do it all on their own, of course, and they don't have to be an expert on oncology or parking, but they will set the tone and the priorities. They will have to develop relationships with all the stakeholders. They will have a job that is not unlike that of premier, mayor or prime minister.

How could anyone think it doesn't matter, that they are all the same?

In 2003 the Iraq War began with the US-led invasion of Iraq. Days before the invasion Prime Minister Jean Chrétien announced that Canada's military would not be part of the mission. The leader of the opposition, Stephen Harper, supported the mission outright and said that Canadian troops should be there.

Whatever anyone thought at the time, a war was about to start and one leader believed we should stay out of it and another leader wanted to go all in. Lives were on the line.

The 45 percent of Canadians who didn't bother voting in the previous election because "they are all the same" were, as always, wrong.

I have to say, and I say this at the risk of destroying any credibility I may have, that I have liked the majority of politicians I have met in my lifetime. Of course we need better people always. That has been said since the beginning of time. But I know for a fact that there are many good people in the racket of politics. People who work long hours for all the right reasons and very little reward.

For every egomaniac drawn to the business for only that reason, there are perhaps six others who work selflessly.

For every person who tries their best to do the very least, there are half a dozen who are the exact opposite.

Politics is no different than any other racket. They say a few bad apples can spoil the lot. That's not entirely true—you can always throw out the few bad ones and save the rest. But it is true that the few bad ones can turn your guts and put you off apples for a while.

We have all seen our fair share of bad apples, but we can't use that as an excuse to ignore the fruits and vegetables. And I am including the Green Party in that analogy.

I say politics has always been my baseball. Perhaps a more accurate description is to say that when it comes to politics, I am like a Toronto Maple Leafs fan. I am used to being disappointed, but for some reason I have decided that I will not give up on them. I see flashes of greatness all the time. And I see potential.

And I know politics matters.

Northern Ontario. After fishing and skinny-dipping with Bob Rae. Bob's a great guy whose caucus leans to the left.

(above) *Shooting with Prime Minister Paul Martin. Between set-ups he wanted to "use the big camera" because he "needed something to fall back on"— turned out he was right. He now shoots second camera on* Breakfast Television.

(left) *Shooting with my late MP the Hon. Jack Layton. He espoused many socialist ideas, but it was me who got the complaint letters—for not wearing a helmet.*

WHO APPROVED THIS MESSAGE?

January 25, 2011

I n politics, attack ads used to be the exception to the rule.
And campaign ads outside of a campaign were completely
unheard of. And now, both exceptions are the new normal.
Canadians are no longer allowed the luxury of sitting down
and watching an episode of *Heartland*—a lovely story about a
girl and her horse—without being bombarded with a
doomsday voice telling us that Michael Ignatieff taught at
Harvard. Which, according to the Conservatives, is worse than
punching a nun.

Now, don't get me wrong—I don't care if they go after
Ignatieff over some policy that he might have. Have at him!
I just can't believe, after all these years, they're still harping on
about the fact that he worked outside of the country. And I take
this personally because I'm from Newfoundland. And like a lot
of Newfoundlanders, when I became an adult, I went away to
work. In fact, I have worked away from Newfoundland for
about as long as Michael Ignatieff worked outside the country.
And if Stephen Harper ever looked me in the eyes and said,
"You're not a Newfoundlander," I think my head would
come off.

Or better yet, I would love to see him say that to, say,
Gordon Pinsent, because who doesn't like to sit back and
watch an eighty-year-old man slap the hell out of someone
half his age?

Negative ads are depressing. I don't care who makes them.
And at the end of the day, the entire country suffers because
it drags the entire political process right down into the toilet.
So if we are going to borrow every horrible political tactic
ever developed in the United States, let's take another page

from their book. Because at least in the United States, if one party attacks another party, the leader responsible has to pop up at the end and say, "I'm Joe Blow and I approve this message." In Canada, our leaders don't do that. And my guess is they never will. Because that takes courage. And bullies generally have none.

SENSE AND SECURITY

November 30, 2010

The holiday season is fast approaching, and this is the time of the year when our thoughts turn to airport security. Because it seems that the media and the federal government are suddenly obsessed with the ethics of the full-body scan and the so-called invasive body search. Which, I believe, is a totally inappropriate term. Let's face it: Anyone who has turned forty and had a routine medical exam understands that nothing that happens at the airport should be described as invasive.

It is very simple: If you want to get on a plane, you have to go through the metal detector, and occasionally, if you're lucky, you get sent to the extra-special touchy-feely line. And when that happens, you go into the body scanner and then, ten seconds later, you're done.

Yes, it does produce an anonymous, semi-naked image of your body. But do you know whose rights I believe are being violated here? The guy in the basement who has to look at those images for twelve hours a day. I mean, have you ever looked around an airport or a bus terminal in this country? Canadians are a wonderful, proud, lumpy northern people—and we look best with our clothes on. So I don't know what that guy in security did in his past life, but he's paying for it now.

Of course, if you don't want the body scan, you can opt for the pat-down. And again, I pity the person who does that for a living. I have witnessed rude and aggressive behaviour at airport security more times than I can count. And 99 percent of the time, it is us, the morally outraged travelling public, that are at fault. Look, if you don't like to be touched, take it up with your therapist or your member of Parliament. Because remember, the government makes the rules here, not the folks in the rubber gloves.

So this holiday season, let's say everyone just calm down, remove the coins from our pockets and let security do their job. Because when they do their job, we get home safe.

NEVER FORGET

November 9, 2010

Canadians are very good at respecting Remembrance Day. If you've ever been lucky enough to attend a ceremony in person, or even watch it live on TV from Ottawa, you know it's not something you'll ever forget. It doesn't get much more moving than that. But for most Canadians, it's a workday, it's a weekday, it's a busy day like any other. It can get away from you.

Last year, I wasn't at a ceremony. I wasn't watching TV. I was squeezing in a haircut. I looked down at my watch and it was two minutes to eleven. Two minutes to the moment where the entire country chooses to be silent, to reflect on the sacrifice of our war dead. And where am I? I'm wearing a giant bib, there's a woman in one ear, telling me she met Rex Murphy in person and he's really quite handsome, and there's a guy in my other ear, telling me how his appendix exploded. And the music is on full blast. And I ask you: Is this why they died on the beaches?

Well, yes it is, actually. So all of us could go about our busy lives without a care in the world. And so I stepped out on the sidewalk, where it was quiet. And then I came back in and the woman said to me, "Did you go for a cigarette?" And I said, "No—it's November 11, it's eleven o'clock, I wanted a moment of silence." And do you ever have those moments where you just want to take back what you just said? Because as soon as I said it, I felt like the biggest holier-than-thou jerk who ever walked the Earth, and she felt worse. Because she didn't mean to forget. It just happened. It can happen to any of us, and we know it shouldn't. So this year, let's make sure we remember . . . to remember. By setting your alarm—it's in your phone. And if you don't know how that works, ask your kids. They can show you how your phone works. And you can tell them why we can never forget.

KEEP AN EYE ON MPs

March 23, 2010

Canada's twenty-second prime minister, Stephen Harper, did something truly historic this past week. He did something that no Canadian prime minister had ever done before.

He went on YouTube and answered questions.

Granted, by YouTube standards he's not as popular as, say, a cat that can flush the toilet, but the fact is he embraced the new media, and for that he should be commended. Because I believe now, more than ever, that it is the internet that can help save Canadian democracy. And it needs saving. And not from any outside forces, but from the people we have so tragically elected. Because believe me, they're out of control.

Kids on field trips go into Question Period, having learned in school that democracy is something worth dying for. They leave an hour later convinced that blithering idiots rule the world. And can you blame them? Anyone who has watched Question Period live knows the evidence is on display. The problem is, Canadians at home can't see that, because all of the bad behaviour is hidden off camera. And the solution is webcams. Regular, old-fashioned webcams, the same kind that many of our younger members of Parliament, like Pierre Poilievre or Jason Kenney, probably have in their homes. There should be one on every desk in the House of Commons. And the minute that place opens up, those cameras should be on.

And we should be able to go online, click and watch our MPs. You know, kind of like a fancy baby monitor. If they're missing in action, like Michael Ignatieff was all last week, we should be able to stare at the empty seat and come to our own conclusions. If they want to sit there and twitter about who's wearing what, like Lisa Raitt, or just sit there and bark like a rabid dog, like John Baird does when he's in a good mood, we should be able to watch that too.

Believe me, after one week of webcamming, they will be on their best behaviour. And who knows, maybe something might even get done.

Because nothing inspires a politician to greatness like a good old-fashioned shaming.

HERE'S TO TEAM CANADA

February 9, 2010

Some people see the glass as half-empty, other people see the glass as half-full. I see the glass and blame the Prime Minister. I'm what you might call a cynic. I can be cynical about anything, even the lead-up to the Olympics.

Not that it was hard. In certain Ottawa circles, it's been a parlour game to sit around guessing how many medals our Olympians have to win in order to guarantee this government a majority. Mother Teresa would become cynical listening to that.

But that said, once the Games begin later this week, I am in. For starters, the entire world is going to freak when they see how beautiful Vancouver is. See, we forget, we take this for granted, but British Columbia, that's one sexy-looking province. Seriously, I expect some Germans' heads will pop right off. Japanese too.

And then there are the athletes. Really, it's all about them—the 206 members of Team Canada.

Now, I'm very lucky. I have a job that's allowed me to meet a lot of Olympians and a lot of Paralympians. But even if I live to be a thousand, I will never understand these people. I have never in my entire life come close to being as committed to a single thing as they are to their sports. And God knows they don't do it for the money. Most of them still live under the poverty line. They work harder than anyone I have ever met in my life, and they do it because they love their sports and they love their country. It can make the most committed cynic believe the glass is half-full.

So with just days to go before the opening of the 2010 Winter Games in Vancouver, here's to the members of Team Canada. You own the podium already.

POLITICAL PROPS

January 26, 2010

C anadians have been very generous to Haiti. People in this country have given an incredible amount of money. But once again, it's members of the Canadian Forces who are doing the heavy lifting. Because really, by the time most of us realized just how dire this situation was, by the time most of us sat down at our laptops and made a donation, a thousand Canadian soldiers were already on their way to Haiti.

And a thousand more show up this week. Imagine if that was your job: Just drop everything and go to hell on earth with no idea when you'll be coming home to your family. I don't know what it's like where you work, but people at the CBC complain when the elevator's on the fritz. But that's soldiers for you. That's what they do. And that's why we admire them.

And that is why soldiers make the perfect political props. In the old days, politicians loved to get their pictures taken with babies. These days, it's soldiers. Which is why, this past July, three hundred Canadian soldiers were given a mission. They were told to drop everything and show up at Canadian Forces Base Gagetown, in uniform, in front of the cameras and clap and cheer as the Minister of National Defence announced that this government was finally buying them new armoured vehicles, which we know they so desperately need.

And so it was perfect timing this past week, when every headline was dominated by the humanitarian crisis in Haiti, that the government let it slip out very quietly that the purchase of armoured vehicles is now on "permanent hold," or what a civilian would call "cancelled." Turns out it was just a photo op, and perhaps a new low in Canadian politics.

You know, it's one thing for the government to order soldiers to put their lives at risk for Canada. That's their job. But to drag them out and use them as a political prop, that's going too far.

At least babies can scream or throw up on a politician. Soldiers don't get that option.

HOW TO USE AN ESCALATOR

December 1, 2009

Every now and then, an issue comes along that transcends politics, that transcends all socio-economic realities. And sometimes the truth needs to be said, no matter how painful that truth may be to some people. This is one of those times, and this is it:

Just because you are on an escalator, that does not mean you have to stop walking.

Up or down, it is an escalator; it is not a ride at Canada's Wonderland. It was designed to keep people moving faster. Which is why it's called an escalator, not a slowthingsdown-alator. And if you must stop on an escalator—because you've got bad knees or you're just a much calmer person than me—you have to stay to the right. The left lane is a passing lane. That means you cannot put your shopping bag there. That also means your best friend cannot park there and talk to you about why you really should have bought that blouse at Value Village. Do you know why? Because when you do that, everyone behind you wants to kill you. And I only bring this up because I am a calm and rational person, but I if I ever go to prison it will be because of something that happened on an escalator. Either that, or near the front doors of a shopping mall or an airport.

Okay, we all know that sometimes big buildings are overwhelming. That does not mean that you get to walk through the front door and just stop and look around for three minutes. If you need to get your bearings, the rules of the road apply here. You must pull over. Find a wall—you can spend all the time you want over there. And while we're on the subject, if you get in an elevator before letting people off an elevator, that should be a criminal offence. With mandatory sentencing.

I don't know why they don't teach this stuff in schools.

Look, we are heading into the holiday season, people. There are going to be big crowds. It's stressful enough. "Peace and goodwill" is the standard wish for the season; that's only going to happen if everyone keeps moving.

HEIR TODAY

November 17, 2009

So the future King of Canada, Prince Charles, and his wife, Camilla, have left our shores and returned safely home to Britain. And sticking with that long-held Canadian tradition of absolute politeness, practised at dinner parties all over this great land, we can talk freely now that the guests of honour have finally left.

Thank God that's over with. Why is it when the Royals pop in for a visit, we're expected to drop everything? And we do—the prime minister of Canada, the governor general, all the TV networks. In fact, the only people who didn't show up this time were the crowds.

This royal visit began in an empty stadium in St. John's, Newfoundland, and went downhill from there. And believe me, if the Royal Family can't fill a stadium in Newfoundland, a place where some people still fly the Union Jack, there's a serious problem. The Tragically Hip can fill that room four nights in a row, and they charge admission.

I know what's going on here. Canada is the "B" circuit. It's just like when I was a kid, and the World Wrestling Federation said they were coming to town. Did they send the Macho Man, Randy Savage? No, instead they sent some drunk guy in tights named Gary.

That's the way the Royal Family views Canada. Look at Prince Harry—*there's* a superstar. They sent Prince Harry to Lesotho for two and a half months. And what do we get? Eleven days with Camilla and a bill for a couple million bucks.

Look, Canada is 142 years old and we still pledge allegiance to a family that lives in a castle in England. No hard feelings, nothing personal. It's time we grew up.

DON'T PANIC
November 3, 2009

There's no doubt about it. At this point in time, it's clear: This country is under attack by a highly contagious virus. And I'm not talking about the swine flu here—we've got a vaccine for that. I'm talking about good old-fashioned fear.

I've never seen anything like it. This past week, we had thousands of people lining up outside a clinic for five hours when they were told there was no vaccine inside. Do you know who lines up for five hours in the cold? Thirteen-year-olds looking for Jonas Brothers tickets. Rational adults do not do that. And it's not even our fault. Canadians are terrified. And in times of crisis, we get our information from the media and the government. Which is ironic, because we don't trust either of them. And look at the media. Last week, every time you turned on the news, the anchor was saying, "Oh my God, there's an outbreak at a Toronto hospital. Outbreak, outbreak, outbreak!" And then they happen to mention, "Oh, by the way, *outbreak* is a technical term. It means three people have the flu."

No, no, no, no. We know what "outbreak" is. It's a Dustin Hoffman movie about a monkey that bites a dude and then his head explodes. In fact, it's two and a half hours of a guy's head exploding. So the media's not really helping us out on the whole panic front.

And then there's the government. Sure, it would be nice if the government stepped up to the plate, but to be fair, it is very busy coming up with advertisements telling us what a great job it's doing with the whole shovels-in–the-ground thing. Apparently, you can only advertise so many things at once. So it looks like we're on our own. But that's okay, because Canadians can beat this thing. All we have to do is put our minds to it. Because unlike the flu, panic is all in our head.

HOW COULD HE HAVE KNOWN?

October 13, 2009

There was really only one story in Ottawa last week. The champagne corks that were popping out of the Prime Minister's Office could be seen from outer space. Stephen Harper has hit the magic 40-percent approval rating, which means a majority government is now within his grasp.

What I find astounding is that the Tories attribute this success not to his piano playing but to his economic record. This is confusing to me because it implies that somewhere it's been recorded that he's doing a good job. I mean, let's not forget, this is the same prime minister who, twelve months ago, told us we could never go into a deficit because there could be no recession as long as he was in charge.

Now of course, hindsight is 20/20. Which is why, if you ask Tories about what Harper said, they all say the same thing. They say, "Ah . . . well . . . please . . . How could he have known we were in a recession?" Well, he could have read a newspaper, or asked my mother, or spoken to a cab driver, but I guess, barring that, they're right. He just didn't see it coming. So instead, we went from zero to the largest deficit in Canadian history. Sixty billion dollars in one year alone.

The good news is that the same guy who said we could never go into a deficit now says we will pay off that $60 billion without raising taxes or cutting spending.

Imagine for a moment your fiancé comes home and tells you that when you weren't looking, he or she dropped 150 grand that you don't have at the casino. Now imagine that the same fiancé says, "Don't worry. We'll pay it back without making a single change to our lifestyle . . . I stand on my financial record." I think, piano playing or not, we'd all start looking at other options.

Now, don't get me wrong—just to be clear to my Tory friends, I am not saying that I believe Michael Ignatieff is better suited to manage this economy. I'm saying that, based on the past twelve months, Porky Pig is better suited to manage this economy.

As it stands right now, this country has a $60 billion wake-up call coming, and for the record, not a single leader has come even close to being honest.

OBAMA'S EXAMPLE

January 20, 2009

It's inauguration day in America, and like everyone else, I can't help but get caught up in the moment. As a Canadian, I did not believe in my lifetime I would see a man like Barack Obama become president of the United States. And not because he's black, but because he ran a positive campaign and actually got elected. And if recent history has taught us anything, it's that that could never work up here.

When it comes to politics, we haven't seen anything remotely positive in a very long time. Think about it. In the last American election, the defining themes were "change is possible" and "hope." And they had the highest voter turnout in forty years. In our last election, the defining themes were "stay the course" and "destroy the enemy." And we had the lowest voter turnout in our entire history.

Clearly, we are on two different tracks. Which is fine—we are a sovereign nation, we are unique on the world stage. For example, we're now the last nation on Earth that wants Guantanamo Bay prison to stay open, and it's not even our prison.

Yes, it's a brave new world, and we're old school. That doesn't mean we shouldn't celebrate the new president—everyone loves this guy. Cripes, when Obama announced that his first foreign visit was going to be to Canada, Stephen Harper looked so excited, I thought his head was going to pop off.

I don't blame him. I'd like to get my picture taken with Obama too. And clearly, the fact that he's visiting Canada is very exciting, because as of today, he is the forty-fourth president of the United States—and eight hours in, he's doing a bang-up job.

He got that job by doing something that no Canadian political leader has done in a very long time. He appealed to the very best in his fellow citizens and gave them something to believe in. So when the visit finally happens, let's hope some of that rubs off.

SNOW TIRES

November 25, 2008

I'm one of those Canadians who like winter. Sure, I think it lasts too long, but still I like to see it coming. So when we had the first snowfall here in Toronto, I went for a walk. And with the snowflakes gently falling against the streetlights, I wandered around the city for about half an hour and enjoyed the sights and sounds of thirteen fender-benders in nine languages.

Yes, it was a winter wonderland, interrupted only when some guy in an Audi locked up his brakes and slid headfirst into a telephone pole about three feet from my legs.

Then he jumped out and said, "Don't move! I might need a witness." And I'm thinking, "What's he need a witness for? What's he gonna do—say it wasn't his fault, that the pole jumped in front of his car?" And then, when I asked him later if he had snow tires on, he looked at me like I was an idiot and said, "I don't need snow tires—I've got all-season radials."

This is what I want to know. How can a guy be smart enough to have a job that lets him drive a fifty-nine-thousand-dollar car and be stupid enough to say he doesn't need snow tires when he's standing next to his Audi that's wrapped around a pole? This is Canada. There's no such thing as all-season tires, just like there's no such thing as all-season footwear. There is in southern California. They're called flip-flops. You wear them in all seasons up here, you'll end up with no feet.

The first sign of flurries in Toronto, the entire place becomes a bumper-car track. No exaggeration—the provincial police said there were nine hundred fender-benders in Toronto in the first five centimetres of snow. This is a crisis, Ontario. There's no shame in being a have-not province. But being a can't-drive province—that's just embarrassing.

Driving in the snow is like sex. If you want to avoid accidents, abstinence is the best policy. But if you're going to take a spin, use protection.

WHO'S IT GONNA BE?

October 28, 2008

I n these uncertain economic times, it's nice to know that some things do not change. The leaves turn. The snow falls. And then there's a Liberal leadership convention.

The smart money says this will be an epic battle between Michael Ignatieff and Bob Rae. Some sort of unavoidable, preordained fight to the death that was first prophesied in ancient scripture. And if the entire party is destroyed in the process, then so be it. Which is why a lot of Liberals are once again looking for that long-shot candidate who can sneak up the middle and stop them all from being annihilated. Justin Trudeau. Will he run? I have no idea. But I know this: mere mortals such as you or me cannot believe the pressure he is under to run. A lot of Liberals out there, they see Justin Trudeau and they go mushy in the head. And when you tell them he has no experience in politics, they say, "It doesn't matter. He grew up around it." Now, this I understand. My father worked for the Department of Fisheries and Oceans for twenty years, and I cannot tell you how many times complete strangers have suggested that I should be put in charge of turbot fish quotas.

And then there's Gerard Kennedy. *Hi, remember me? I'm the guy who gave you Dion.* Now for the Liberals to go with Kennedy at this point . . . that's a bit like necking with the guy at the office Christmas party that gave you the cold sore—twice. But hey, stranger things have happened. And then, of course, there's the dream of the white knight. Will a Frank McKenna just show up out of the blue and save the party? Now, this is interesting, because usually, in most countries, when they're talking about dream candidates, they throw around adjectives like *brilliant, charismatic, dynamic.* Whereas in Canada, only one adjective counts: bilingual. Yeah, Barack Obama wouldn't cut it up here.

But to any Liberals out there who can't make up their minds, I say, don't worry—at the rate your party is going, with three leadership conventions in five years, eventually, everyone's going to get a turn.

SCARED STUPID BY SCIENCE

February 19, 2008

When twenty-year-old Ellen Page from Halifax got an Academy Award nomination for best actress, we all cheered. When our hockey team won gold at the World Junior Championships, we all cheered. You don't have to be a movie fan or a hockey fan to be moved by this stuff. You just have to be a Canadian.

And likewise, you don't have to be a genius to be very proud of the fact that Canadian scientists won the Nobel Peace Prize. I mean, this is the mother of all prizes. In fact, they gave one to Mother Teresa.

So, what happened this past week when those winning Canadian scientists came to Parliament Hill for a reception in their honour with their Nobel Prize tucked beneath their arms? Prime Minister Harper, the guy whose job it is to represent us at these things, refused to attend. The Canadian cabinet refused to attend. And why? Because these scientists, who—I don't know if I've mentioned this or not—won the Nobel Peace Prize, had the gall to do it by formulating a plan to fight climate change. And my guess is it doesn't call for an increase in oil sands production. So, as a result, not a single cabinet minister would cross the hall and shake the scientists' hands.

Remember, this is the same government that just recently fired the national science adviser—a guy whose job it was to advise the Prime Minister and cabinet on all issues pertaining to science. They just didn't see the need for that guy. With this crowd, being a science adviser is a bit like being the Maytag repairman. The phone just doesn't ring.

What I want to know is: How did we get here? Canadian scientists gave humankind the polio vaccine. We discovered insulin. Heck, we even invented the Robertson screwdriver. And suddenly science is the new enemy.

I understand that in politics, people and parties have enemies, and destroying your enemy is the name of the game. That's the way you win. But we cannot allow the government to declare war on knowledge. Otherwise, we all lose.

Unless, of course, they start passing out Nobel Prizes for idiocy.

APOCALYPSE SNOW

December 4, 2007

Canadians love to talk about the weather—always have and always will. It's what we do. We have always been passionate about the weather, but we have never been hysterical about the weather, and certainly, we have never been afraid of the weather. But suddenly, that seems to be changing.

At first, I thought this was a Toronto thing. Because when you move to Toronto you realize pretty quickly that when it comes to the weather, there are two parallel universes. There's what you hear about in the media, and then there's what you see out your window. You can wake up and turn on the news and see a lead story about a snowstorm that slammed the city, how there were three hundred accidents between five and nine in the morning, how no flights took off. And the reporter on the scene is so panicked, he sounds like he's reporting live from the bottom of a collapsed mine shaft. And you think, "Oh my God, I had no idea. Those poor people."

But then you realize: Hang on, I'm *in* Toronto. And you look out the window and see there's three centimetres of snow on the ground and the kid on the street walking a dog is wearing a T-shirt.

There was no snowstorm. There was no weather bomb. There were flurries. And then it got windy and the entire city ground to a halt. But before the rest of the country gets all cocky, know this: Weather hysteria is spreading across this nation like some sort of demented low-pressure system.

We don't have forecasts anymore, we have weathertainment. It's designed to scare the hell out of you. Cold weather and snow are now reported as though it was raining frogs or there was a plague of locusts out there. Problem is, cold weather is

not a sign of a coming apocalypse. It's just business as usual in
Canada. But tell that to the crowd at the Weather Network.
If you listened to them for five minutes, you wouldn't leave
the house for five months.

This is the true north strong and free, and cold and wet and
icy and dark—sometimes all at once. It's why God invented
long johns. This is Canada. We have winter. Embrace it.

IT DOES GET BETTER

November 27, 2007

Last week was National Bullying Awareness Week in
Canada. Now, for those of us long out of school, it's
tempting to treat that one like National Nutrition Week
and ignore it altogether. But unfortunately, if you Google
"bully," "Canada" and "suicide," you'll get more hits than if
you were searching for "Paris Hilton" and "hotel room."

And we're not talking about one or two horror stories
here—we're talking about hundreds. And the more of these
stories you read, the more you realize the greatest thing about
being an adult is that, no matter how bad things get, you never
have to go to grade nine ever again. Because for a lot of kids out
there, going to school doesn't rank right up there as the best days
of their life. Because they're different in some way, they look at
going to school like some sort of prison sentence. And you can't
blame them. I mean, you walk in the door when you're five years

old, they keep you for twelve years. You're not allowed to leave. Cripes, in this country, you do less time for murder.

Of course, the minute you leave school, you immediately forget how bad it can be for some people. But you want to say to these kids who are being bullied, "You know what? You're right. These are not the best days of your life. In fact, these are probably the worst. But after this, they get better, and then— believe it or not—they get great. Trust me: I'm one of the smartest guys I know."

And if you're being hassled because you're a geek—in a few years, you will inherit the Earth. The biggest geek I went to school with was seventy-six pounds; he got hassled every day. The poor guy couldn't walk up a flight of steps without falling over to the left or getting a nosebleed. I have no idea how he got through it—in hindsight, he is the bravest man I know— but these days he's as happy as Larry. He runs a video game company in California. If I had his money, I'd burn mine.

And if you're being harassed in school because you're gay, the fact is, in a few years you will have more friends than you know what to do with. You can be as open as you want. Not only will you be the funniest guy in the room, but when you fly standby on Air Canada, you'll get a free upgrade to business class. Because the guy behind the counter? He's gay too.

So if you're being bullied in school because you're different, please tell someone about it, and remember: Even in a real prison, eventually, everyone gets parole.

Pierre Berton:
That's How He Rolled

THEY WERE CALLED Celebrity Tips—a series of instructional
videos starring Canadian icons.

In the early years of the *Mercer Report*, some of the nation's
most famous people appeared on the show, demonstrating
simple, often mundane but crucial skills.

How does one safely boost a car battery? Every Canadian
should know how to do that. And who better to teach the
nation than the most glamorous woman I have had the
privilege of knowing: Ms. Shirley Douglas.

Shirley was thrilled to take part. And so the daughter of Tommy
Douglas, the famous actress, activist and member of the Order of
Canada, grabbed the booster cables and taught the nation.

It was thirty below, her hair was impeccable and she refused
to wear a hat. It should be noted for the record that she needed
absolutely no direction when it came to the issue of which
cable went where.

When she finished, she said, "While we are here, would
you like me to show you how to change a tire?"

Celebrated novelist Margaret Atwood appeared in a Celebrity Tip to teach Canadians how to stop a hockey puck. I will always remember standing on location, in a hockey rink, with the author of *The Handmaid's Tale*, explaining to her that her line about "protecting your five-hole" was an actual thing and not a double entendre.

Geddy Lee, the lead singer of Rush—considered by millions of Canadians and Latin Americans to be the greatest rock and roll band in the history of the world—taught us the importance of toboggan safety.

Yes, thanks to my job, I got to go tobogganing with Geddy Lee in the park by my house. Scratch that off the bucket list.

The problem with the Celebrity Tips, I discovered, was that in order for them to work, the celebrity had to be much more than a celebrity. They had to be an icon. And the thing about icons is that there aren't a lot of them around. We were running out fast.

And then there was the matter of convincing these people to do something perhaps outside of their comfort zone— NHL enforcer Tie Domi gave tips on how to set a pretty Thanksgiving table. Tie is the kind of guy who is up for anything, but not everyone is quite so self-deprecating.

Ever since the tips began, we had always tossed around the notion of producing one entitled "How to Roll a Joint." We never put any real thought into the logistics because, for the life of me, I could not think of a single Canadian icon who might be prepared to go on TV and roll a joint.

As I said, Celebrity Tips was an item in the early days of the show, as you can tell from the fact that we were even considering including one on joint rolling. This was before we realized that with our high ratings, we had inadvertently become a family show. We were thrilled when we got the data that showed college students were watching in droves.

And we knew adults were watching too. But when we found out that entire families and small kids were a part of our growing audience, that changed a few things.

We loved the idea that families were watching together, and Gerald and I decided that while we wouldn't change the show, we would be careful to avoid embarrassing parents or kids while they watched together. That meant no jokes that might lead to conversations like "Mommy, what does autoerotic asphyxiation mean?"

These are the sacrifices we make for prime-time television.

But in the early days, I did find myself saying with regret, "We are never going to find someone famous to go on TV and teach people how to roll a joint."

It was Gerald who said, "Pierre Berton might."

I have long since given up figuring out how Gerald knows some of the things that he knows. He has better show business instincts than anyone I have ever met. But in this instance I was pretty sure he had taken leave of his senses.

Pierre Berton was not just an icon, he was an icon's icon.

He was Canada's first celebrity author. He wrote important books. A lot of them. I had four feet of them on my shelf. He was the reason I became enamoured with Canadian history. If it weren't for Pierre Berton and the *Heritage Minutes*, most of us in Canada would be like goldfish—no idea where we came from or where we were going.

I said with authority, "There is no way Pierre Berton is going to come on the show and roll a joint."

Gerald said, "Give him a call. I heard that back in the day he liked a puff."

Remember, while this was no longer "back in the day," this was still thirteen years before any credible political figure in Canada was actually using the phrase "legalize it."

The prospect, no matter how slim, of booking Pierre Berton was too tempting. So at the risk of embarrassing myself in an encounter with someone I admired so much, I gave him a call.

Tracking famous people down to ask them a favour involves breaking through the lines of defence—publicists, managers, husbands, wives and protectors. It takes time and patience.

Reaching Pierre Berton was not hard. He was listed in the phone book.

I had remembered reading a profile on him years earlier in which he talked about his days as a columnist for the *Toronto Star*. For many years he was the most-read opinion columnist in Canada's largest newspaper. He was often controversial, often cantankerous and wildly opinionated. He wrote the kind of columns that made people angry. And when he wrote something he knew people would complain about, Berton would say, "You don't like it? Call me. I'm in the book."

Throughout his entire career this most famous Canadian was reachable by any Canadian who could read or dial 411.

That was a different time. The drummer for Great Big Sea has an unlisted number to this day, and they broke up six years ago.

It was the end of the day and I went downstairs and got in the van. A young man by the name of Nik Sexton was driving. Nik was a new addition to the team. How he came to be with us is a classic Newfoundland tale. I knew Nik's mother. Gerald knew Nik's mother. Gerald had worked with Nik's uncle, the late Tommy Sexton, on the CBC comedy show *CODCO*. Tommy was one of my comedy idols. I had known Nik since he was five.

Nik had come to Toronto from St. John's to attend film and TV school. For whatever reason, Nik decided it wasn't for him and dropped out before the tuition cheque cleared. Nik admitted that he was somewhat embarrassed that he hadn't stayed in school, and rather than head back to St. John's he decided he was going to stick around and make it on his own in the big city.

In that classic St. John's way, Nik's mother, Mary, said, "I'll call Rick and Gerald," which she did. Gerald said, "There is always a place for Nik," and he came on board. He started as a production assistant. In television this can mean many things, but it is almost always what is politely called an "entry-level position."

On this day I sat in the van and prepared to contact Pierre Berton. Nik was behind the wheel.

I dialed 411. "A number for Pierre Berton, please. Kleinburg, Ontario."

Nik said, "Pierre Berton? Dude with the bow ties?"

This is when I knew that Pierre Berton and *only* Pierre Berton would be perfect for this tip. It was too good. He was a ninety-year-old historian and the nineteen-year-old skateboarder sitting next to me knew who he was.

The robot voice gave me the number and I dialed.

He picked up on the first ring.

"Hello."

"Hello, it's Rick Mercer calling. Is Pierre Berton there, please?"

"Yes, Rick, hello. This is Pierre. What can I do for you?"

"Well, Mr. Berton, first of all, let me tell you I am a huge fan. I read *Tales of the Klondike* in high school, and then *Dieppe*, and then *Vimy*. I have many of your books. I just bought your latest a few weeks ago. But the reason why I am calling is, we have a segment on our show called 'Celebrity Tips.' Famous people come on and teach Canadians how to do things—"

205

"I am aware of the segment," he said. "I saw June Callwood kick a field goal last week."

"Yes, why yes, you did," I said. "I was hoping *you* would come on the show and . . . well . . . do a tip."

"I see. And what would I be teaching people to do?"

This was the make-or-break point.

"Well, Mr. Berton, you would be teaching Canadians how to properly roll a joint."

Nik gave me a thumbs-up.

There was a pause.

"Go on," he said.

"Uh, well, honestly, that's it. I mean, that's the whole bit. You are Pierre Berton and you teach us to roll a joint. Nobody would ever expect you to do that, because, well, you're Pierre Berton."

He said, "I like it. Come to my house tomorrow around ten."

This was the best news and the worst news. The best in the sense that he was actually going to do the segment. The worst in that he said he wanted to do it the next day. TV doesn't work like that.

"Oh, Mr. Berton, no. We couldn't possibly do this tomorrow. I was simply checking to see if you would consider it. We need to book a crew, and I need to write the thing, and we have to figure out how to get people to the location. We can probably arrange a time next week."

"Well, there's no guarantee I'll be here next week."

I realized he wasn't talking about perhaps taking off for Florida. This was what is called a cultural emergency. Extraordinary measures were necessary.

"Mr. Berton, you are right. We will figure it out. We will be at your house tomorrow at 10 a.m. It should take a few

hours at most."

"Okay," he said. "One thing, though: you bring the weed."

Now, *this* I hadn't thought of. The weed!

"Right, of course. Well, I guess I will talk to our props department or our art department and we will figure something out—"

"No," he said. "If I'm going to roll a joint on TV, I won't be rolling oregano. People will know the difference. It will look ridiculous."

Well, far be it from me to allow an icon to look ridiculous on my show. Part of my entire philosophy was ensuring that anyone who ever appeared on the show looked great, be they an icon or an oyster fisherman.

"One second, please," I said.

I covered the phone and said to Nik: "Nik, when you pick me up tomorrow morning, it will be like eight or something. Do you think you could, I don't know, bring a bag of weed?"

Nik didn't bat an eye. "I can do that," he said.

Nik fixed problems from the moment he showed up. He was an excellent hire. He stayed with the show for fifteen seasons, working his way up to associate producer. He also directs and writes feature films.

The next day, the very next day, at exactly 10 a.m., I knocked on Pierre Berton's door.

He opened it and he looked just like himself. Elegant, somewhat frailer than I had expected, but resplendent in a jacket and bow tie.

"Welcome to my home," he said.

It was a lovely house. Bright, airy, very comfortable and very lived in. Dripping in books and art. It was exactly where you would imagine a famous author would live.

After the warm greetings, Burton got down to business. He said, "Did you bring the weed?"

Pierre Berton was amazing to work with. He was a gracious host. He welcomed me and the small crew with open arms. There is an adage in our business: "Never let a film crew in your home." I guess, as with the listed phone number, Pierre Berton never got that memo.

The finished product is my favourite celebrity tip. In it, he teaches Nik (now promoted to special skills extra) how to roll the perfect joint. As his rolling surface, he chose the cover of his latest book, *Prisoners of the North*. No fool he. Pierre Berton was always a master at selling books, and he had not lost his touch.

He never once forgot his lines. He was sharp. He entertained us with stories. And he was complimentary about the show and the rants. As he was one of the original great shit disturbers, this meant the world to me.

He signed all the books I had dragged along from my bookshelf and posed for pictures with everyone on the small crew. He told me that he was thrilled that his last TV appearance would be on the show and that it would probably cause some controversy.

"It's ridiculous," he said, "that so many young people have had their lives ruined because of small-possession charges."

I, of course, assured him this would be far from his last TV appearance. But as so often before in his life, he was right. It was his last TV show. He passed away six weeks after it aired, *Prisoners of the North* still on *The Globe and Mail's* best-seller list.

On my list of people that I was truly thrilled to meet, Pierre Berton is at the top.

And on the front porch as I was leaving, I got to thank him not only for the day, for being a gracious host, but for everything he did, including opening my eyes to Canada's history.

"You are very welcome," he said.

And I will never forget the last words this true Canadian icon said to me. He looked at me dead in the eye and said:

"Rick, leave the weed."

Short-arm selfie.

Why did I wrap up the show after fifteen seasons? The truth is, being on the road was just too much work. Exhausting.

With the Surf Sister Surf School in Tofino, BC.

John Marshall and me on the top of Mount Nimbus, BC.

TARGETED EQUALLY

December 5, 2006

The debate over same-sex marriage is back.

I see this as a positive development. Where did Canadians get the idea that, once a minority's rights are defined, they are somehow set in stone? It's time Canadians woke up and realized those days are long gone. This is an era of reflection.

Sure, the Charter looks nice hanging on a wall, but the fact is, it grants far too many rights that are contrary to the deeply held personal views of many chubby white guys.

I hear rumours that the Conservatives plan on devoting every Thursday in the House of Commons to more votes on minority rights. Their list of motions so far includes debates on whether the Chinese should be allowed to drive, whether women should be allowed to vote and whether turbans should be allowed in elevators that travel more than sixteen floors.

In order to ensure that all minorities are targeted equally, the Conservatives have come up with an ingenious way of creating motions.

This year, in lieu of a Secret Santa exchange, every Tory has to write on a slip of paper the name of a minority that bugs them. On the back of the slip they must write a so-called "right we all enjoy." The slips will be mixed up and placed in a gorgeous, festive ballot box decorated by John Baird for the occasion. At this year's Christmas party, each member will be blindfolded and asked to draw a slip of paper out of the box. That slip of paper is their own present and Canada's too. Imagine the hilarity that will ensue when Justice Minister Vic Toews stands up and says, "This year, my Christmas gift is a motion to debate whether Hindus can own property in New Brunswick."

I can hear the laughter from here.

NATION INSIDE A NATION

November 28, 2006

You have to hand it to Stephen Harper—the man is on a roll.

The Tories like to say that Harper is good at his job because, above all else, he is a master chess player. In one bold move, he stood up in the House of Commons, embarrassed the Bloc and protected his own seats in Quebec. And all he had to do was table a simple motion that says that from now on, the Government of Canada recognizes that the Québécois form a nation inside a nation.

So all you kids in grade three can forget what you just learned about Canada being ten provinces and three territories. We are now nine provinces, three territories and a nation inside a nation.

When you write this down, kids, you might want to use a pencil. Because there's going to be a lot more nations to learn about. Take the Cree in Quebec. Clearly, *they're* a nation. Well, actually, they're a nation inside a nation inside a nation. Imagine you are a Cree person who is gay, who cheers for the Blue Jays and who lives in Montreal. You'd be a member of